CELESTIALLY AUSPICIOUS OCCASIONS™

☆ ☆ ☆

SEASONS, CYCLES
& CELEBRATIONS

CELESTIALLY AUSPICIOUS OCCASIONS^T

Seasons, Cycles & Celebrations

Donna Henes

URBAN SHAMAN

Illustrations by Joonhee Lee

A PERIGEE BOOK

For additional copyright and permissions information, see p. 233.

Portions of this book previously appeared in slightly different forms in the author's newspaper and magazine articles.

A Perigee Book
Published by The Berkley Publishing Group
200 Madison Avenue
New York, NY 10016

Copyright © 1996 by Donna Henes
Book design by Irving Perkins Associates
Cover design by Wendy Bass
Cover and interior illustrations by Joonhee Lee

First edition: July 1996

Published simultaneously in Canada.

The Putnam Berkley World Wide Web site address is
http://www.berkley.com

Library of Congress Cataloging-in-Publication Data

Henes, Donna.
    Celestially auspicious occasions : seasons, cycles, and
    celebrations / by Donna Henes ; illustrations by Joonhee Lee.
        p.   cm.
    Includes bibliographical references.
    ISBN 0-399-52210-7
    1. New Age movement.   2. Seasons—Miscellanea.   3. Cycles—
Miscellanea.   4. Holidays—Miscellanea.   5. Mythology.   I. Title.
BP605.N48H45   1996
299'.93—dc20   95-46029
                                                                      CIP

Printed in the United States of America

10   9   8   7   6   5   4   3   2

For Adelaide, my past.
For Daile, my present.
For Shameike, the future of us all.

CONTENTS

☆───────────☾

ACKNOWLEDGMENTS

☆————————————(

There
How shall I go to compose this important song
How shall I invent it to help me
I am wholly ignorant
There
Those who have great facility to invent songs
Those who dance with elegance
Those who know the beautiful old chants
I will get inspiration from them
There

Ogpingalik
(Twentieth-century Netsilik Eskimo)

I wish to state from the start that I am a ritualist, a ceremonialist, an urban shaman, and much of what I know, I know by heart. What I am not is an astronomer, a historian, a theologian, an anthropologist, an archaeologist, a folklorist, a biologist, a psychologist, a physicist.

This book is full of brilliant bits of information and fabulous facts researched and written by illustrious thinkers in every field without whom I would have been lost. I bow down to them with utter respect. Particularly useful were Merlin Stone's *Ancient Mirrors of Womanhood*, volumes 1 and 2; Barbara Walker's *The Woman's Encyclopedia of Myths and Secrets* and *The Woman's Dictionary of Symbols and Sacred Objects*; and Anthony Aveni's *Conversing with the Planets* and *Empires of Time*, all of which I drank like water. I strongly encourage readers to pursue these and the other wonderful works listed in the bibliography.

My Thanks

To my trusty team: Linda Brown, who has worked by my side and on my behalf through thick and thin; Carl Lundi, who is always there when I need him; and Melvin Jenkins, my right- and left-hand man. Their caring support has made a daily difference.

To my agent, Donald Lehr, for being so generously behind me from the start, and to Karen Marshall for putting us together in the first place.

To Joonhee Lee, the illustrator, who rose to the occasion with great aplomb. It was a delight to collaborate with such an openhearted, open-minded soul.

To my editor at Perigee, Sheila Curry, for her clarity and insightful understanding. To June Balish and Stephany Evans, my past editors at *Free Spirit*, for their invaluable encouragement and critique.

To Susy Chippindale, Director of the Planetarium at the Santa Fe Community College, and Dr. Neil de Grasse Tyson, Director, American Museum Hayden Planetarium, New York City, for being so giving with their time and information.

To Jeannie Belhobec of the Cuyahoga County Library System, Cleveland, Ohio; Jenny Sweetland of Gale Research, Inc., Detroit, and Dave Bianco, Omnigraphics, Inc., Detroit, for research assistance.

To Sabra Moore and Leslie J. Laufer for photographic advice and assistance. To Tabitha Tarosian for computerizing me.

To all the thousands of children in the New York City Public School System with whom I have shared my workshop, Faces of the Seasons™. The natives of sixty-some countries, they have offered me frank feedback and fresh perspective on the seasonal cycles and celebrations around the world.

To all my extended ritual circles who have enriched and inspired me on Celestially Auspicious Occasions over the past twenty years and have kept my mailbox full with clippings of fascinating scientific and folkloric tidbits.

To the marvelously knowledgeable and insightful women of the ever-incarnating Goddess study group: Christina Biaggi, Charoula Dontopolous, Rosemary Dudley, Gail Dunlop, Mary Beth Edelson, Buffy Johnson, Mimi Lobell, and Merlin Stone. Those evenings of free-wheeling information exchange, inspiration, and emotional support resulted in many extraordinary books. A toast to us all.

To Jerri Allyn, Miriam Bird, Alison Rosa Clark, Skipper Edwards, Geraldine Hannon, Daile Kaplan, Helge Krarup, Barbara Malmet, Dominique Mazeaud, Lucienne Muller, Omar Ruffin, Rosemary Schultz, David Silberberg, Kay Turner, Bé van der Heide, and Suzanne Zuckerman, my loyal cheering section; to Tashene Keith (RIP), Tommy Sullivan (RIP), and James Vaughan (RIP), my guardian aliens; to my Bud and Ola, kindred spirits; and to Shameike Thomas, who stroked my head when the computer began to eat away my brain.

To Sybil, who speaks.

CELESTIALLY AUSPICIOUS OCCASIONS™

SEASONS, CYCLES
&
CELEBRATIONS

FROM THE FILES OF A CONTEMPORARY CEREMONIALIST:

*Explorations of Cross-Cultural Ritual Practice
and the Natural Phenomena That Inspire
and Inform It*

INTRODUCTION

Throughout human existence, people have plotted and marked the passing of time. The ability to correctly track the cycles of nature gave the advantage of being able to effectively plan and prepare for the future. Knowing with some certainty when the birds and herds migrated and when they could be expected to return, when the fruits ripened and the grasses grew, when the nuts were ready for gathering, when the river rose and flooded, when the rains came, when it was likely to get cold again, meant survival.

From the earliest ice ages there are examples of crude calendrical reckonings, bone and stone renderings of the regularly occurring astronomical cycles: the phases of the moon, the ascendance and changing position of certain stars and constellations, the daily and annual disappearance and reappearance of the sun. Incised, chipped, carved, and painted, these symbols attest to the astute observation skills of our ancestors.

The special days that announce the advance and retreat of the sun, moon, and stars were not merely noted, they were celebrated—marked by ceremony as well as graven in stone. The recurrence of these Celestially Auspicious Occasions served as significant milestones with which people were able to measure the cycle of the seasons and the seasons of their lives. Ultimately, people kept track of time in order to live in tune with it.

Living in attunement with the workings of the world means to consciously interact and to engage viscerally, sensually, and spiritually with it. To assume an active awareness of personal response-ability. For people who live in intimate association with the elements, people who, indeed, identify themselves as integral partners with the forces of nature, celebration is a friendly act of faith.

Each dawn and each dusk, each rising and setting of the moon and stars, each cycle of the sun, the approach of each season, is met with reverence and awe. The planets are actively encouraged in their rounds by the practice of supplication, sacrifice, prayer, promise, and thanksgiving. This ritual participation in the cosmic process both affirms and assures the continuation of the cyclical order of time.

Though few people in our crowded cacophonous urban world live in such focused alignment with the earth, the holidays we celebrate are the legacy of these oldest seasonal observances. In some cases, the days are still holy, the original intentions and primal power of the occasion still manifest. In most cases, however, the shell of the celebration has been maintained, while its soul has been modernized, sanitized, secularized, and commercialized beyond recognition, their original function forgotten.

The indigenous peoples of the world, by clinging tenaciously to the sanity and wisdom they have inherited, maintain their perception of a universe in which everything is intricately and inextricably interconnected. When Pueblo Indians run up the mountain at dawn on the Summer Solstice, they are not just greeting the sun. They are, by their very participation, helping the sun to rise.

This sanctified collaboration with the cosmos creates a consciousness of a sacred reality which endures in many tribal communities throughout the world even today. During the course of the calendrical research for this book, I spoke with Doris Leedercharge at the Lakota Sinte Glesko College on the Rosebud Sioux Reservation in South Dakota. I told her that I was anxious to include as many Native American holy days as possible, and she replied, "According to our religion, every day is holy!"

It is this transcendent recognition of the sacred, this transformation of vision, that allows the inherent, hidden divinity in all things to become apparent. We, alas, as a culture, have lost the ability, the facility, the talent, for such crystal insight. It is our challenge as hectic, driven people to charge our common dailiness with that same transcendent clarity. Our reward is to see the ordinary as special and the special as extraordinary.

It has been my great pleasure to gather and select some of the special days, holidays, holy days, and Celestially Auspicious Occasions of many cultures and traditions. As numerous as they are, they represent but a small sampling of the richly diverse smorgasbord of ceremony celebrated around the globe. Their number is sufficient, however, to remind us that every day, somewhere, someone is celebrating something. That every day is most certainly holy.

And while it is this very diversity that makes our world such an endlessly interesting and deliciously exciting place, it is the underlying similarities, the strange and wonderful convergences of cross-cultural ritual practice, that point to the sameness of the human condition the world over. By celebrating these Celestially Auspicious Occasions we commit ourselves to that universal connection; we follow our own roots back to their common source, that primal spirit that connects us all at our cosmic center.

☆————————————☾

PART I

Celestially Auspicious Occasions

THE GREAT ROUND

The circle of time, the round of the seasons, surrounds us and encompasses us. All there is, was, and will be exists within its spinning circumference.

Everything the Power of the World does is done in a circle. The sky is round, and I have heard that the earth is round like a ball and so are all the stars. The wind, in its greatest power, whirls. Birds make their nests in circles, for theirs is the same religion as ours. The sun comes forth and goes down again in a circle. The moon does the same, and both are round. Even the seasons always come back to where they were. The life of a human being is a circle from childhood to childhood, and so it is in everything where power moves.

> Black Elk
> (Twentieth-century Oglala Sioux)

Consider the cycles of the systems: the celestial revolutions, rotations, and orbits that collaboratively choreograph the complex ballet of the galaxies; the grand rondeau of the cosmos, their complicated set of machinations together creating time. Consider the planetary circulation of water through the periods of precipitation and evaporation, freeze and thaw, ebb and flow. Consider the circular exchange of oxygen and carbon dioxide as plants and animals breathe in and out, making air together, like the Eskimo women who make eerie music by blowing on each other's larynxes. Consider the infinitesimally slow buildup and unavoidable breakdown of sand, stone, skeletons, soil, stars, and continental shelves. Ashes to ashes, dust to dust.

Everything is always changing. Nothing is static. Nothing ever stays the same. "Round and round it goes. Where it stops, no one knows." This continuously turning spiral of transformation is reflected in the life cycle of all things. Like the moon, which is new, waxes, is full, and wanes, everything is born, lives, and then dies. Everything.

The circle dance of the heavenly spheres leads us along in its hypnotic rhythm as we reel through space, twirl through time, twist, gyrate, through fate. As the world turns, each subtle shift of season, of atmospheric pressure, each nuance of light and dark resonates in our bodies, our spirits, our entire being. The passage of time is reflected, in microcosm, in our own presence. In the span of our lives, the years, the epochs, the eras come full circle. We ourselves become the cycle.

> *See how whole it all is,*
> *not diminished for a second,*
> *how you age with the days*
> *that keep dawning,*
> *how you bring your lived-out day*
> *as a gift to eternity.*

Jacob Glatstein
(Twentieth-century Yiddish)

The year is a wheel with eight spokes. Each circuit is comparable to the cycle of a human life. The Winter Solstice is the time before we were born, the great dark uterine void from which all is formed. The vast black ring around all possibility, its perimeter bulging with promise. Light is conceived in the cold dark at the time of the Winter Solstice. The smallest spark, the most tentative hint of a glow, is imagined in the dense ambience of its absence. The sun is a mere gleam in the eye of eternity. Light, no matter how tiny, equals life.

A spin of the wheel brings us to Midwinter, six weeks later. It is the halfway marker on the slow road to spring. Life is almost here where we can feel it. Its fresh scent precedes it, coloring the air with anticipation. The earth pulses with underground energy, undulating toward the universal origin. There is a quickening of life inside of Mother Earth as a woman, a cow, a mare, a ewe, a lioness, a she-wolf experiences it—the unbearably dear, heartbreakingly intimate beat of the future in her belly.

Then spring, eagerly awaited and warmly welcomed. Spring bursts forth from the frozen confines of winter, released from its embryonic state of suspended animation, into a waiting world of innocent wonder. The beloved baby-faced season of tender shoots, fuzzy buds, and naked newborns, spring brings the birth, rebirth, resurrection, of all nature. Hope springs eternal.

Midspring starts, spurts, skips, surges, sprints along in a frenzied frolic of unrestrained growth. Nature, like a teenager, is all agog with too many churning hormones. The world in midspring is imbued with an aura of adolescent enthusiasm, the atmosphere charged with vernal effervescence, a vibrant, verdant vitality. The breath of life is sweet with perfumed bouquets of youthful blush which color the cheeks of flowers and lovers everywhere.

The Summer Solstice sizzles with an electric maturity, a practiced adult sensuality. More grounded, rounded, ready, and fertile. Summer is the towering peak of the period of light, the most potent of passionate times. The Summer Solstice is like what a Chicana friend of mine would call *"una mujer en su salsa."* A woman in her hot sauce, simmering with piquant succulence.

Midsummer brings on a menopausal change of life. It's suddenly a little too hot, a little too dry. Flushed. In midsummer we see a world ripe with abundance which is just starting to show its age. Although the season is still spry, it's becoming a bit strained, a mite frayed around the edges. A wrinkle here and there, a gray hair or two, the first few fallen leaves. Terrifying intimations of mortality.

At the Autumn Equinox, Mother Earth comes into her cronedom, fulfilling her cycle by going to seed. The experience, the passion and pain of an entire lifetime, the fruit of all labor, is ready to be harvested now. In the fall, the wisdom of the ages is winnowed and milled. Wholesome bread is baked from the grains of time and stored in big baskets for the future.

By Midfall, the end is in sight. The end of the light, the end of the year, the ultimate and inescapable end of it all. By now most of nature is dead or looks that way. Everything has migrated, hibernated, or become brittle and bare in the growing chill and dark. Here the cycle reaches its completion. And we prepare to begin again at the ending.

> Death matters, as does life. As it ends it begins again. Knowing that is both my comfort and fear. Perfection is a long road; I shall never see its end—the ribbon of life winds back on itself.

> *Awakening of Osiris*
> (Second-century-B.C. Egyptian)

The circle is perhaps humanity's first and most elemental symbol. It stands for the whole: the circumference and all contained therein. The cosmic womb and the vulvic opening to its divine source of energy. The creation myths of many lands speak of the great round, the cosmic egg, the bubble, the spiral, the moon, the hoop, from which the world originated. The circle is breast, is swollen belly. The circle is the shape of the relationship in which we are universally joined.

Combining as it does the projected authority of the heavenly forces with that of the female form, the circle confers a concept of a potent creatrix, our first deity. It might even be said that the Great Round was our first religion. From the beginning, in reverence, in deference, to Her, people invoked the protection and sense of unity of this primordial image. They inscribed, described, circumscribed, their lives, their customs, and their surroundings with circles.

Prehistoric matrifocal cultures (as well as contemporary tribal societies) built round houses with circular hearths. Vessels were round, as were granaries, fences, pens, livestock enclosures, burial mounds, ritual grounds, ovens, and wells. Circular architecture is stronger, more attractive, and more efficient and economical since it uses fewer materials to create a greater volume of space. Villages, and ultimately towns and some great cities such as Paris and Washington, D.C., were designed as radiating circles.

> O *Wakan-Tanka*, behold Your pipe! I hold it over the smoke of this herb. O *Wakan-Tanka*, behold also this sacred place which we have made. We know that its center is Your dwelling place. Upon this circle the generations will walk.*
>
>   Black Elk
>   (Twentieth-century Oglala Sioux)

Consecrated sites of public worship—sacred groves, temples, standing stone circles, and medicine wheels—were cast in the round. Magical circles were drawn in rock, in marble, in earth, to delineate and focus the divine powers of the cosmos. When folks danced in ceremonial manifestation of the celestial cycles, it was also in a circle. And when measures of defense were called for, ranks were drawn in to form a sealed, protective ring.

The circle has indelibly permeated philosophical thought, religious ceremony, and ritual practice. Reincarnation is understood by vast multitudes of people everywhere to be the way in which we participate in the everlasting continuous circle of life. The related Eastern concepts of Karma and the Western Wiccan law of a three- or seven-fold return, point the way for placing personal response-ability on a universal scale. Or "what goes around, comes around."

By historic times, the potter's wheel was in wide-scale use and the wheeled chariot had been invented. These worldly applications of the holy circle had profound effects on civilization. The written languages of many cultures have recorded a com-

*From *The Sacred Pipe: Black Elk's Account of the Seven Rites of the Oglala Sioux*, recorded and edited by Joseph Epes Brown. Copyright © 1953 by the University of Oklahoma Press.

plex vocabulary uniting the sacred and profane associations of the circle as time, heavens, order, power, and awe. In Sanskrit, for example, the word *mandala* means "circle, globe, round, ring, orb, halo"; also "group, band, multitude, collection." The word *cakra*, "wheel," refers to a potter's wheel, a discus, or a chariot as well as the zodiac. One of the strongest images in the Rig-Veda is the fiery solar chariot that carries the sun on his journey across the sky each day. Apollo, too, drove a sun chariot.

Ancient Egyptian hieroglyphs picture the circle and its variations as a pregnant symbol full of spiritual as well as practical significance. The circle stands for the cosmos and its time-producing cycles: "sun, sunshine, daytime, rise, New Year's Day." It refers to fertility and production, as in "placenta, threshing floor, village, netherworld. And it relates these powers to light, site, sight, and insight, as in "eye, wakeful, weep, realm of the king, the sun god, Ra."

The Greek root for "circle" was derived from the name of the *kirkos*, "a hawk who flies in circles." Related to and extending the meaning of "circle" are words that refer to anything round, such as "eyeball, Cyclops [round eye], drum, shield, the walls around a city, a place of assembly, the vault of the heavens." In Latin, *circulus*, a diminutive form of *circus*, which means "a circular figure or ring," also refers to "a circuit of time."

> *From point comes a line, then a circle:*
> *When the circuit of this cycle is complete,*
> *Then the last is joined to the first.*

Shabistarî
(Fourteenth-century Persian)

Because its perimeter is unbroken, the circle also represents time, which has no beginning and no end—but always implies a cyclical return. A circle renders a dependable ordering of existence. Constancy. Stability. Infinity. Eternity. Long before they were able to precisely plot the actual circular paths of the planets and stars, people pictured the cosmos and its regenerative powers as circular.

The concept of time as a circle is quite widespread. In the third millennium B.C., the Sumerians identified a girdle of twelve constellations along the ecliptic path traveled by the sun, moon, and planets. These were used as solar-monthly markers. Over time, and with additional influence from Babylonia, Egypt, and Greece, they developed into the now-familiar zodiac. Mesoamerica, India, China, and the rest of the Far East also have circular astrological systems for keeping track of time.

As early as 2500 B.C., the Indians of the Rocky Mountain region laid out huge circles of stones in the grassy valleys. These ceremonial medicine wheels had twenty-eight spokes with a twenty-ninth center pole—which equals the number of days in a lunar month. The famous Aztec circular calendar was cut from a stone eleven feet in diameter in the fifteenth century A.D. Both of these New World timepieces were designed by cultures that did not use the wheel in the course of their ordinary endeavors.

Clocks with circular faces are still popular today, despite advanced digital technology. We still gather in circles and rings for ritual spectacles such as circuses, rodeos, car, dog, and pony races, sporting events, children's games, and theater productions. We still refer to our closest compatriots, friends, and family as our circle. And when we are feeling threatened, we still circle our proverbial wagons in unconscious invocation of the protective powers of the omnipotent cosmic round.

What we have lost, however, is the ability to think in anything but a straight line. Our culture associates straight with "good and correct." We try our best not to go in circles. We stand straight. We fly straight as an arrow (phallus). We are straight talking. We look someone straight in the eye. We shoot straight from the hip. We keep our affairs, our rooms, and the parts in our hair straight.

The Judeo-Christian-Islamic concept of time is linear. Time is seen as *history*—that is, *Homosapien*-centric—concentrated on the events that occur to, or are caused by, men (by which I mean males), rather than on the eternal cycles of everlasting return, the larger-than-life movements of the circular universe. The perception of time promulgated by a historical perspective is that events rush ahead, one following the other, in single file until time eventually runs out.

Consequently, we are always thinking, planning, pushing ahead, in a great huff of a hurry. We forget that there will always be a *mañana*. In Western civilization, the art of circular thinking is, for the most part, a completely impover-*rushed* one. The gesture we make when we mention someone mentally odd is quite telling, don't you think? We put a finger next to our ear and make incessant circling motions.

Yet during the centuries when pioneering Europeans were hacking and whacking their way through the American wilderness, they were thought to be quite mad by the resident tribes. You can always tell where the white men have been, they would say, because they leave everything they touch—houses, roads, cultivated fields, fences—in neatly arranged straight lines. And as if they weren't weird enough, they dance square dances. One of the more vivid memories I have from a visit to Israel is the way the meticulously planted forests march, tree after tree, row after orderly row, in perfectly disciplined phalanx, over the hills of scattered stones and scrub.

> *Remember, remember the circle of the sky*
> *the stars and the eagle*
> *the supernatural winds*
> *breathing day and night*
> *from the four directions*

Remember, remember the life of the great sun
  breathing on the earth
  it lies upon the earth
  to bring out life upon the earth
  life covering the earth

Remember, remember the sacredness of all things
  running streams and dwellings
  the young inside the nest
  a hearth for holy fire
  the sacred name of fire.

"Invoking the Powers" (Hako)
Pawnee, Osage, Omaha

There simply aren't all that many straight lines in nature. So why do we want them so desperately in our minds? Having our heads screwed on straight makes it practically impossible for us to take a good look around. It seems to me that if we are to repair the rent in our disconnected, disrespectful, and dysfunctional relationship with nature, we are going to have to throw off our "straight" jackets and start thinking like she does.

THE WINTER SOLSTICE

O Radiant Dawn, splendor of eternal light, sun of justice;
come shine on those who dwell in darkness and the shadow
of death.

"O" Antiphon vespers (December 21, Winter Solstice)
from *The Liturgy of the Hours*

Come the fall, there is no denying the apparent disappearance of the sun. The rays of light become ever more indirect as they skim overhead at an almost horizontal angle, their energy and warmth barely reaching us below. Their glow is weak and wan, a diluted wash. Insipid. Depressing.

The Winter Solstice, the shortest day and the longest night of the year, is as dark as it gets. The sun is now at its nadir, the farthest southern limit of its range. And there it seems to want to stay for a while. At the solstice, the sun rises and sets at the same time for several days. The length of the daylight hours remains the same. *Solstice,* in Latin, means "the sun stands still." It has stopped retreating and yet hasn't begun to come back. It hovers in pregnant hesitation before it gets back on track again, resting before it begins its annual return trip across the equator into the Northern Hemisphere for its homecoming. Back to us.

Tromsø, Norway, population 40,000, situated on the Arctic Coast just two hundred miles south of the Arctic Circle, is the farthest-north settlement of any size in the world. The winter sun sets there in November and doesn't rise again until late January. This sunless period is called by the citizens *Mørketiden,* "the murky time," and is marked by dramatic increases of mental instability, physical illness, domestic violence, suicides, arrests, alcoholism, drug abuse, and diminished school performance. One resident reported, "*Mørketiden* brings out the worst qualities in people: envy, jealousy, suspicion. People get tense, restless, and fearful. They become preoccupied with thoughts of death and suicide. They lose the ability to concentrate, and work slows down. People talk about the light constantly and long for the sun to come back."

During the solstice for us in the temperate zones, it's dark as well. It's dismal. It's cold. It's bleak. And winter is only about to begin. It will be long months before we can expect to smell the advance of spring in the air again. But the consolation is that though the cold season is just starting, the sun has now turned its face toward us and has begun its return approach. The light will return in its wake, increasing constantly so that by the Vernal Equinox the light of day is once again equal to the dark of night. And it keeps increasing until the Summer Solstice, when again the sun stands still—this time at the northern pinnacle of its path.

And so the cycle continues. The sun and the earth traveling together, turning, circling, spinning through space. The earth and the sun, ever engaged in a cosmic back-and-forth, give-and-take, do-si-do dance of dark and light, day and night. A veritable cha-cha-cha of beat retreat and eventual return. An again-and-again samba for all seasons. An eternal waltz played in annual time.

> *In winter I get up at night*
> *And dress by yellow candlelight.*
> *In summer, quite the other way,*
> *I have to go to bed by day.*

Robert Louis Stevenson
(Nineteenth-century Scottish)

But in the meantime it's damn dark out there. The days have shriveled to a skeleton flicker of light. The frozen nights are endless. These are dim, drab times. No flowers, no foliage. No insects, few birds. No animals out and about. The earth itself is congealed with cold. Dark death and arctic gloom surround us. How do we know that the sun, too, won't die, its flame of life extinguished forever? How do we know that it won't just go off and leave us, abandon us to the night?

We know because it always has come back. And because we have, to the best of our abilities, computed that it always will (at least for the next 5 billion years). We can see the seasonal cycle of light and dark through the scope of thousands of years of the accumulated astronomical data—observations, investigations, calculations, and collective experience—of many cultures. We know with fair certainty that day follows night, spring follows winter. We are quite confident, secure in the sure return of the faithful sun. We haven't the slightest conscious doubt.

But wrapped in the dark womb of the weather, we can easily imagine the terrifying prospect of the permanent demise of the sun and the consequent loss of light, the loss of heat. The loss of life. Without the comfort of the familiar cyclical pattern, the approach of each winter with its attendant chiaroscuro like the disturbing dark shadows of an Ingmar Bergman film, would be agonizing. The tension intensified by the chill.

With the death of the sun, the world would be cast back to the state that it occupied before creation, the classical concept of chaos. The black void. The Great Uterine Darkness. It is from this elemental ether that the old creatrix goddesses are said to have brought forth all that is. Tantric sages refer to this condition as the Great Goddess in her aspect of "dark formlessness when there was neither the creation nor the sun, the moon, the planets, and the earth, and when the darkness was enveloped in the Darkness, the Mother, the Formless One, Maha-Kali, the Great Power, was . . . The Absolute."

The sacred spark of creative potential contained within the primordial womb is one of humanity's oldest concepts. The visual symbol that represents it, a dot enclosed within the circle, is also extremely ancient. Still in common use today, it is the astronomical notation for the sun. The spark supreme.

Among the most archaic images of the sun is that of the brilliant radiance that clothes the Great Goddess. The Great Mother of the pre-Islamic peoples of southern Arabia was the sun, Atthar or Al-llat. In Mesopotamia she was called Arinna, Queen of Heaven. The Vikings named her Sol, the old Germanic tribes Sunna, the Celts Sul or Sulis. The goddess sun was known among the societies of Siberia and North America. She is Sun Sister to the Inuits; Sun Woman to the Australian Aruntas; Akewa to the Tobas of Argentina. The sun has retained its archaic feminine gender in northern Europe and Arab nations as well as in Japan. To this day, members of the Japanese royal family trace their shining descent to Amaterasu Omikami, the Heaven-Illuminating Goddess.

According to legend, Amaterasu withdrew into a cave to hide from the irritating antics of her bothersome brother, Susu-wo-no, the storm god. Her action plunged the world into darkness and the people panicked. They begged, beseeched, implored the sun goddess to come back, but to no avail. At last, on the Winter Solstice, Alarming Woman, a sacred clown, succeeded in charming, teasing, and finally yanking her out, as if from an earthly birth canal, and reinstating her on her rightful celestial throne.

Other cultures see the goddess not as the sun herself, but as the mother of the sun. The bringer-forth, the protector and controller, the guiding light of the sun and its cycles. According to Maori myth, the sun dies each night and returns to the cave/womb of the deep to bathe in the maternal uterine waters of life, from which he is reborn each morning. The Hindu fire god, Agni, is described as "he who swells in the mother."

It is on the Winter Solstice, the day when the light begins to lengthen and regain power, that the archetypal Great Mother gave birth to the sun, who is her son. The great Egyptian mother goddess, Isis, gave birth to Horus, the sun god, on the Winter Solstice. On the same day, Leto gave birth to the bright, shining Apollo, and Demeter, the great Mother Earth goddess, bore Dionysus. In Rome, the shortest day was also the birthday of the Invincible Sun, *Dies Natalis Invictis Solis,* as well as that of Mithra, the Persian god of light and guardian against evil. Christ, too, is a luminous son, the latest descendant of the ancient matriarchal mystery of the nativity of the sun/son. Since the Gospels do not mention the exact date of his birth, it was not celebrated by the early church. It seems clear that when the church in the fourth century A.D. adopted December 25 as his birthday, it was in order to transfer the heathen devotions honoring the birth of the sun to he who was called "the sun of righteousness."

According to the mythology of the peoples of the Pacific Northwest, the sun was held captive by a selfish old chief. When Raven, the trickster hero, saw that the people were forced to live in darkness, he turned himself into a pine needle and floated down to earth, landing in a river. When the daughter of the chief drank from the river, she swallowed the pine needle and became pregnant and gave birth to a son, who was Raven in disguise. The baby boy began to cry and would not stop. In order to placate him, his grandfather, the chief, gave him a ball of light to play with. As soon as Raven had the ball in his hands, he flew back up to the sky with the light ball, where he installed it so that the people could have light.

> *I arise from rest with movements swift*
> *As the beat of a raven's wings*
> *I arise*
> *To meet the day*
> *Wa-wa.*
> *My face is turned from the dark of night*
> *To gaze at the dawn of day*
> *Now whitening in the sky.*
>
> Iglulik Eskimo,
> Canadian Northwest Territories

A common theme of solstice ceremonies everywhere is the burning of fires to symbolically rekindle the dwindling sun. People gather together to cheer on the ascendancy of the light.

The victory of the very forces of life. The Hindu Festival of Lights, Divali, comes about six weeks before the solstice. The story surrounding Divali is that Lord Rama, the hero of the Hindu epic *Ramayana*, was sent into exile (read darkness), but he redeems himself by slaying the evil ten-headed demon King Ravana, who had stolen his wife, Sita, the light of his life. He is then, after fourteen years, able to return home in triumph.

On Divali, people light his way back into the fold each year and, at the same time, invite the gifts of the goddess of prosperity and plenty, Lakshmi. They place clusters of *deyas*, small clay lanterns filled with oil and a burning cotton wick, along all the pathways, garden walls, windowsills, and patios in a town or village, where their flickering glow provides a warm welcome.

Chanukah, the Jewish Festival of Lights celebrated near the Winter Solstice, commemorates a miracle that is a metaphor for the dwindling, then returning, light of the season. The popular story goes: The stock of oil used to fuel the everlasting light on the altar of the temple ran low. A one-day supply was all that was left, but it was able to continue burning for the eight difficult days that it took the citizenry under siege to procure more. The eight-day Chanukah ritual involves the lighting and blessing of eight candles in a *menorah*, a ceremonial candelabra. One additional flame is kindled each night, mimicking the gradual gathering of light in the dark sky. For Jews, the candles represent the light of truth, the flame of freedom.

Throughout northern Europe, where the weather is more severe, the solstice fires were lit indoors. The Yule log and colored-light decorations that are today emblematic of Christmas are the same as were once lit in honor of Sulis, Sol, Sunna, the old goddess of the sun. In Sweden, Santa Lucia, St. Lucy, St. Light, is observed on December 13, the date of the Winter Solstice on the old Julian calendar. Young girls dressed in white nightgowns with crowns of lit candles in their hair parade the streets at dawn, waking people with coffee and fresh-baked cakes in the spiral shape of the many-spoked sun wheel.

Kwanzaa is an African American holiday that has been celebrated during the solstice season since 1966, when it was first conceived by Dr. Maulana Kerenga, a black studies professor and cultural nationalist. Although it is inspired by African harvest and thanksgiving festivals—Kwanzaa means "first fruits" in Kiswahili—it is celebrated like a solstice fire festival. A major ritual element is the lighting of seven red, black, and green candles in a *kinara*, or holder. Each candle stands for the Seven African Principles, fundamental precepts upon which a creative, productive, and successful community life is based: *Umoja*, unity; *Kujichagulia*, self-determination; *Ujima*, collective work; *Ujamaa*, shared economics; *Nia*, life purpose; *Kuumba*, creativity; *Imani*, faith. Beginning on December 26, the candles are lit alternately from left to right, one each night, until they are all aglow.

With the recognition that the solar light in the sky makes it possible for there to be life on earth comes sincere response-ability. As the sun energizes our lives, so, too, must we return energy skyward at the solstice when the winter light is failing. As Mother Teresa counsels,"To keep a lamp burning, we have to keep putting oil in it." Now we must ask not what the sun can do for us, but rather, what we can do for the sun. It becomes imperative, in fact, to do all that we can to entice, aid, abet, and ensure the safe return of the sun to earth. Life depends on it.

> *Now this day,*
> *My sun father,*
> *Now that you have come out standing to your sacred place,*
> *That from which we draw the water of life,*
> *Prayer meal,*
> *Here I give you.*
>
> "Offering to the Rising Sun"
> Zuni

In both imperial China and pre-Columbian Peru, it was the holy duty of the emperors to personally assure the continuation of the cosmos through their annual performance of ritual sacrifices to heaven on the Winter Solstice. After fasting for three days they would each emerge before the winter sunrise and proceed to the top of the Round Mound in the Temple of Heaven in Beijing and to Haucaypata, Cuzco's ceremonial plaza. There, before retinues of their peoples, they offered libations and obeisance to the celestial center of the universe. They knelt, they bowed—the Inca blew reverent kisses—to the supreme solar source of all light.

The king of Swaziland in South Africa, the incarnation of the sun himself, retires in seclusion for the period preceding the solstice. Then, on the day of the sun's return, his warriors dance and chant in front of his compound, urging him to emerge from the dark. The Mayan Indians of Guatemala perform a flying pole dance, *palo voladare*, in honor of the old, indigenous pre-Columbian sun god. Two dancers climb a fifty-foot pole to the energetic beat of a flute and drum. At the top, each wraps one end of an attached rope around one foot and leap off into the wild blue yonder. If they manage to land on their feet, the sun god will be pleased enough to start sending more light to earth each day.

Soyal is the Winter Solstice observance of the Hopi Indians of the American Southwest. During this sacred season of solar renewal, the kachinas, the spirit helpers of the tribe, emerge from their dark kivas. They come up from the underground ceremonial spaces to join the community for the six-month period of ascending light. Fires are lit and the original creation tale is retold, reenacted, and reclaimed. This ritual participation in the process of the universe affirms and assures the continuation of the cyclical order of time. At Soyal, the sun is symbolically, ceremonially, turned on its course back to the people, thus renewing life for all the world.

The return of the retreating sun, which retrieves us from the dark of night, the pitch of winter, is a microcosmic re-creation of the origination of the universe, the first birth of the sun. The Winter Solstice is an anniversary celebration of creation. It is both natural and necessary to join together in the warmth of community to welcome the return of light to a world in the dark and to rekindle the spirit of hope in our heart.

Lighting a light at the darkest time of the year is a pledge. A promise. A sacred vow. Such a small, symbolic gesture. So elegantly simple. So significant. Each tentative flicker of each tiny flame is a reminder of the fragility and pulsating persistence of the life force. Each spark, a signal flare of faith.

> *O Sun, source of light, love and*
> *power in the universe*
> *Whose radiance illuminates the whole Earth,*
> *illuminate also our hearts*
> *That they, too may do your work.*
>
> Sanskrit prayer for peace

MIDWINTER

Nothing in the universe has an on/off switch. Movement from one stage of time/life to another is always gradual, progressive, each stage containing a subtle hint, a clue, of the next to come. Slowly shifting light, temperature, weather patterns, and emotions signal the winding down of one season and the impending commencement of the next.

While most people think of there being four seasons, each

one beginning with a solstice or an equinox, this is only partially true. There are, in addition, four celestially energetic pivotal periods of the year that occur at the halfway point of each of the four seasons. These stations are called cross-quarter days. The halfway points serve as sort of semi-seasons, which, if we choose to observe them, help us to perceive and adjust to the changes around and within us.

Although the existence of the cross-quarter days is largely unknown, the holidays that have grown up around them are still actively celebrated in our mass culture. February 2, May 1, August 1, and November 1 mark the halfway points of winter, spring, summer, and fall respectively. The current holidays are Groundhog Day, May Day, Lammas, and Halloween/All Saints' Day/All Souls' Day. All but Lammas (known as Second Planting in agricultural communities) are still popular festivals celebrated throughout the United States today. Rooted in ancient pagan and primal observances of cyclical change, these rites have survived through time and retain a strong, if subliminal, resonating relevance for us today.

February 2 marks the winter midpoint. The midwinter cross-quarter day can be likened to the quickening of life, that magic moment when an expectant mother experiences the child within her shift position for the very first time.

The days are perceptibly longer now. There is the faintest breath of a whisper of the coming of spring in the air. There begin to be signs: The first tiny buds, like goose bumps on bare skin, begin to form on naked branches. Snowdrops appear, pushing their fragile blooms up through the still-frosty soil. Hibernating animals begin a restless stir in their underground nests. They toss and turn and awaken enough to devour a midnight meal before turning over and tucking back in again for the duration. It isn't spring yet. But there is the palpable promise. The eager anticipation of the annual resurgence of life that comes each spring.

Winter for most plants and animals is a time of retreat, both physically and psychologically. It is a quiet dark time conducive to deep rest and deep thought when we delve into the depth of the heart of our soul to discover the wisdom and riches buried there.

> *Under the Light, yet under,*
> *Under the Grass and the Dirt,*
> *Under the Beetle's Cellar*
> *Under the Clover's Root.*
>
> *Further than Arm could stretch*
> *Were it Giant long,*
> *Further than Sunshine could*
> *Were the Day Year long . . .*

> Emily Dickinson
> (Nineteenth-century American)

Prophesy and purification are the recurrent mythic and symbolic themes of the midwinter festivals. The concept of prophesy is drawn from the foresight and faith that spring, in all its verdant glory, is on its predictable way, even amid the hard white winter. Purification suggests careful preparations for its coming: clearing the way with the fiery brilliance of insight which comes from visiting the deep, dark internal winter of our souls and seeing therein our own part in the constant and continually changing cycles of life.

In midwinter the land is gripped in death, and Demeter, the ancient goddess of grain and fertility descends to the underworld in pursuit of her lost dear daughter, Persephone. Disconsolate, Ceres explores the far reaches of the territories of Hades and her own private hell, her journey lit by a single candle. The impassioned determination of her search and her ultimate discovery shed the first glimmer of light in the indelible dark of winter. The creative spark of full consciousness. With the light from her candle we can begin to see the spiritual direction of the new cycle.

> *If my torch goes out it will be dark.*
> *Dark life behind the eyes.*
> *My trip with no way back*
> *and this tunnel my tomb.*
> *A tunnel like a mother's stomach.*
> *Her identical architecture.*
> *Her climate of signs and penumbra.*
> *Through this labyrinth until finding it.*

Claribel Alegría
(Twentieth-century El Salvadoran)

In Greece there is an underground sanctuary dedicated to Hades, god of the underworld, and Persephone, his stolen bride. For millennia, pilgrims have made their way to the Nekyomanteion of Ephra, a labyrinthine arrangement of spiral-shaped rooms and passageways carved into the belly of Mother Earth. *Manteion* means "a place in which one hears prophesy," and *nekyo* or *necro* refers to the dead. Petitioners descend deep into the divine womb by way of a serpentine tunnel leading to a cavernous dark chamber which sits above a crypt. There, encouraged by Demeter's resolve, in the unsteady light of just one torch, they consult the oracles of the dead for inspiration, for direction. "It is better to light one candle than curse the darkness" could be their motto.

Midwinter was celebrated as Imbolc by the ancient Celts and also as an early Gaelic fire festival. Both were held in honor of Bridget, a.k.a. Brigid, Bride, Brigetis, the Northern White Goddess, guardian of the home fire and hearth. Fire was the symbol of her white-hot mystic magic. The intense heat of the flame, her fervent faith in the return of the light to the world. Today the day belongs to her spiritual daughter, St. Brigid, adored patron saint of Ireland.

The hagiographic accounts of St. Brigid are few. She was allegedly Ireland's first convert to Christianity and the founder of that country's first convent in the fifth century. She continued to be honored just as the goddess was before her, and the worship of her devotees did not change over the centuries. A holy fire, reminiscent of those kept constantly burning by the worshipers of her earlier goddess incarnation, was maintained at her shrine in Kildare until it was finally ordered doused by the church in the thirteenth century. Until not so long ago, domestic fires were routinely extinguished on her day, February 1, and then rekindled and blessed in a preparatory act of purification.

In Rome, the Midwinter day belonged to Juno Februata, virgin mother of Mars. *Februare*, in Latin, means "to expiate, to purify." Here, too, fires were lit, and candles were blessed and burned in her honor. Women also continued to carry candles in street processions at this same time of year in memory of Ceres' candlelit search belowground. Determined to stop this goddess worship, Pope Sergius I claimed this pagan holiday for the church. Renamed Candlemas, February 2 was to be celebrated as the feast of the purification of the Virgin Mary forty days after she had given birth. The observance, however, remained the same—the blessing and burning of candles for Our Lady of Light.

Two indigenous New World celebrations echo this practice. In Aztec Mexico, all fires were extinguished at the winter midpoint. There followed five dark days during which there was a period of inactivity and sorrowing. Then the Aztec New Year was ushered in with the ritual relighting of the fires, feasting, and festing. During the Iroquois six-day midwinter New Year ceremony, members of the False Face Society visit every home in the community. They put out the fire in each stove, stir up the ashes, and then blow them onto the inhabitants as a curative rite. These purification ceremonies of renewed fire suggest a clearing of humanity's earthly orientation in order to be open to the growing divine light.

> *. . . Now again the smoke arises.*
> *And the people speak through it to you,*
> *Oh you who dwell in the sky!*
> *Now we implore you. May it so occur again when*
> *   the earth warms,*
> *May your desires be fulfilled and your*
> *   descendants once again see your creations . . .*

> New Year's Ceremony
> Seneca Nation of the Iroquois League

Midwinter is when the sun first reappears in Siberia after the months-long polar winter. At this most eagerly awaited, wondrous time, the Nganasani people celebrate the Clean Tent Ceremony, the premier rite of their ritual calendar. A special "clean tent" is erected in the village, and here the shaman sits for three to nine days while the children dance and play outside the tent. Encased in dark isolation, surrounded by the insular sound of her/his heart pulsing in prayers, s/he seeks the guiding light of the spirit and invokes the protection of the god/desses for all the people and the whole of nature for the year to come.

Li Ch'un, "spring begins," is celebrated in the more temperate climate of China during the first week of February as determined by a lunar calendar. At this time, the new almanacs for the year are issued. The people are then informed of the agricultural prospects predicted for the coming year through the means of effigies drawn through the streets. These spring oxen are dressed according to the weather forecasts listed in the almanac. If the head is yellow, they know that great heat is foretold for the coming summer; green tells of a lot of sickness in the spring; red denotes drought; black shows rain; and white means high winds and storms to come.

At this halfway marker of the winter, it is customary in many places to foretell future weather conditions. In Greece, people maintain that whatever the weather on Candlemas Day, it will continue the same for the forty days to follow. The Latin ditty predicts:

> *Si sol splendescat Maria purificante,*
> *Major erit glacies post festum quam fuit ante.*

The Scottish say:

> *If Candlemas day be dry and fair,*
> *The half o' winter's to come and mair.*
> *If Candlemas day be wet and foul.*
> *The half o' winter's gane at Yule.*

The Welsh tell:

> *If Candlemas Day is fair and clear*
> *There'll be two winters in one year.*

In Warwickshire, they advise:

> *If Candlemas Day be wind and rain*
> *Winter is gone and won't come again.*

And in Cumbria, they warn:

> *If Candlemas Day be sunny and warm,*
> *Ye may mend your old mittens*
> *And look for a storm.*

The winter cross-quarter day is also a time of weather prediction in Germany, where farmers claim they "would rather see their wife upon a bier, than that Candlemas Day be sunny and clear." Midwinter is designated Badger Day in recognition of the underground movement toward life, which is manifest in this season. When the first wave of German farmers emigrated to this country, they brought Badger Day with them. But faced with a lack of badgers, the Pennsylvania settlers were forced to substitute the American groundhog.

Each year on February 2, the attention of the nation is directed to Punxsutawney, Pennsylvania, where Groundhog Day is big business. Weather forecasters and news reporters converge to stake out the burrow of this furry hibernating creature in order to ascertain the true prognosis of the coming of spring. Groundhog Day is a direct and thriving descendant of age-old Midwinter divinatory practices like gazing into Bridgid's holy well, or the tunnel leading to the oracle crypt, or Ceres' explorations of the cave. Will Phil, the groundhog, see his shadow? Will spring come on time?

Okay. Now pay attention. This is how it works: If the groundhog sees its shadow, it means that there are *still* six more weeks of winter. If it doesn't see its shadow, it means that spring is *only* six weeks away. Tricky, eh? There are *always* six more weeks of winter. Spring is *always* six weeks away. That is why we mark the day in the first place. To remind us that winter is half over. To assess our situation. According to the *Old Farmer's Almanac*, by Groundhog Day you should still have half of your food store and half of your fuel if you are going to make it through the remainder of winter.

With the first sensing of the coming of spring at midwinter, we find ourselves antsy, anxious to emerge from our inward focus already. We strain toward the annual vernal miracle of rebirth and resurrection. Yearn for the light. But it isn't yet time for spring, and spring *always* starts on time. First we have to finish winter.

At midwinter, we still have six more weeks before we will emerge from the dark. It can't always be light, you know. If we always run in pursuit of the light, we miss half of each day; half of each year. Half of our feelings. Half of our lives. And, besides, there are some things that you can only learn in the dark. As Simone Weil wrote in *Gravity and Grace*, "It is misery, not pleasure, which contains the secret of the divine wisdom."

> *He liked*
> *lanterns and lamps*
> *and*
> *torches and tapers*
> *and*
> *beacons and bonfires*
> *and*
> *flashlights and flares.*
> *But he didn't like the Night.*

> Ray Bradbury
> (Twentieth-century American)

We are like frightened little children who need a night-light. We forget that the light is always there—somewhere—anyway. We just can't see it when it's dark. It's like the dark side of the moon which we perceive only as absence of light, failing to recognize the dark richness of its own ambience, its own energy. Its own invaluable lessons. The dark offers us a chance for enlightenment, but our eyes fail us in the shadows. And so we panic, preferring anything to the pitch, the petrifying recesses, of the truth of our own souls.

This terror is the turning point. The time for determination. It is at this critical moment that we can consciously choose to dwell in the dark for a while longer—for as long as it takes—*despite* our fear. We can decide to take it on and take it in. To deal with it. To go where it takes us. To explore the blind byways of our pain, inching along, feeling our way with our tongues if we have to. To plumb our emotional depths and mine that precious secret ore of our own heartfelt experience. To feel our heart actually break, explode apart, like a geode, revealing the glittering crystals growing inside. To engage passionately in *all* that life has to offer.

At the funeral of Thurgood Marshall, the Reverend Dr. Calvin Butts, pastor of the Abyssinian Baptist Church in Harlem, eulogized, "In order to *get* somewhere, you got to *go through* something."

THE SPRING EQUINOX

If the Winter Solstice signals the birth of the sun, then the Spring Equinox exclaims the birth of the earth and the resurrection from the dark death of winter of the wide world of nature. The life that has stayed hidden, in exile or underground, during the long deep sleep of the season now shifts and starts to stir. Poking and peeking, it seeks the surface. Space. Air. Light. Stretching skyward, bulbs, shoots, and buds burst forth from the earth, exploding open, exposing their tender green growth. The sweet sap rises.

The birth waters break. The skies open. It rains, it pours, it mists. The defrosting sodden soil teems, churns, with every creepy-crawly thing that ever slithered out of a swamp. Hordes of birds descend, drawn by the juicy feast. Animals awaken from their pregnant hibernations, skinny and starving and suckling their young. Birds and beasts set out on a concerted feeding frenzy, gorging themselves and their ravenous, insatiable, mouths-ever-open offspring.

It is as if the great egg of the whole world has hatched. And so it has in the collective imagination and symbolism of many cultures. The myths of the peoples of Polynesia, India, Indonesia, Iran, Greece, Phoenicia, Latvia, Estonia, Finland, Central America, and parts of South America and Africa all describe an original cosmic egg from which the universe is born. The Latin proverb *Omne vivum ex ovo* proclaims, "All life comes from an egg." It is only natural and not so subtle to assign the birth of the world to a Great Mother Goddess who laid the egg of life. All of nature, after all, is a constant cyclical reminder of a fertile female force. The seed source of all generation. All life does, indeed, come from an egg.

> Mother Earth lies in the world's midst rounded like an egg and all Blessings are there inside her as in a honeycomb.
>
> Petronius
> (First-century-A.D. Roman)

The Egyptian goddess Hathor took the form of the Nile goose, the Great Cackler, to lay the golden egg that was the sun. The Egyptian hieroglyphic notation for the World Egg is the same as the one for an embryo in the womb of a woman. The Celts, too, had a Mother Goose who laid the egg of all existence. According to the Hawaiians, the Big Island was produced from the egg of a huge water bird. In various cultures, she was known as the Great Midwife; the Egg Mother; Knosuano, the Moon Egg of Ghana; the Druidic Egg of the World. In Greek Orphic tradition, the Great Goddess of womblike darkness, Mother Night, was impregnated by the Wind, and she gives forth with the silver egg from which the earth emerges.

According to the Chinese, the first human being sprang from the egg that Tien, the controlling principle of the universe, dropped from the heaven into the primordial waters. The Chimu Indians of Peru are descended, ordinary people and heroes alike, from the original egg which is the moon. The Samoan Heavenly One hatched from an egg whose shell pieces became the earth. Prajapati, the creator of all living things in Indian mythology, was born of a great golden egg which was first incubated in the uterine waters of eternity. The god Brahma burst forth from a gold egg. A Hindu scripture relates that in the very beginning the earth was a nonbeing which eventually evolved into an egg. After lying in a state of incubation for one year it split into two parts:

> *That which was silver, became the earth.*
> *That which was gold, became the sky.*
> *That which was fluid, became the ocean.*
> *That which were the veins, became the rivers.*
> *And that which was born therefrom is*
>   *yonder sun.*

The egg has long been humanity's obvious and essential symbol for birth, fertility, eternity. For life itself. Nests of clay eggs have been found in great numbers in Ice Age tombs in Sweden and Russia. Romans and Slavs also left caches of eggs in the graves of their dead. Maoris buried people with an egg in one hand. Kassians placed an egg in the navel of a corpse. A Han dynasty tomb unearthed in Ch'ang-sha, China, was furnished with a banquet table laid with lacquered bowls of eggs, peaches, pears, melons, and rice. Here was a feast to nourish the buried noblewoman on her journey.

Descendants of Jews from eastern Galacia eat eggs following a burial service. Eggs representing the continuation of the generations and the victory of life over death are eaten during the Passover seder, the ceremonial meal that ushers in this ancient spring festival. Another egg, which has been roasted until it is brown and brittle, is not eaten. It is placed on the seder plate in the center of the table in commemoration of the sacrifices in the original Temple in Jerusalem. The hard-boiled adversity which is life. I have heard of one family that uses hollowed eggs rather than roasted. After the seder each year, the mother inscribes the date on the egg and decorates it with symbols. Their Passover egg collection dates from 1812.

In time, the egg, the symbol of life, of birth, came to stand for the season of spring. For it is then that the aspect of fertility and rebirth within the cycle is so overwhelmingly evident. The egg, in fact, *stands at* spring. It actually stands up on its end at the moment of the Vernal Equinox, as the sun crosses the equator into the Northern Hemisphere. Stands in salute to spring.

I discovered this phenomenon soon after I started studying and celebrating the seasons in the city on the Winter Solstice of 1975, when a friend returned from the Orient with an odd bit of equinoctial information. Apparently, in prerevolutionary China, it was customary for peasants to stand eggs on their ends on the first day of spring. To do so would guarantee good luck for the entire year. I have since had people tell me that their Scandinavian grandparents, too, balanced eggs at the equinox in their home countries. I immediately set out to prove it on American soil.

That was twenty years ago, and I have initiated and personally participated in the public balancing of many thousands of eggs—"Eggs on End: Standing on Ceremony"—on every Spring Equinox since. There is something extraordinarily powerful in the image, in the experience, of an egg standing upright. Something incredibly moving that elicits ancient and rarely accessed emotions. The egg becomes the symbol of a new season, the birth of new life. An icon of equilibrium. Eggs on End: Standing on Ceremony is every bit a traditional vernal fertility rite, a popular, contemporary celebration of the return of green and growth and light after the dark winter. The luck engendered by this ritual comes from the act of joyous engagement with nature.

> *Some eggs do it, others do not*
> *stand up for the occasion*
> *on Spring Equinox*
>
> *When ShaMama Donna tell them*
> *to touch base and to rise, some*
> *eggs cool it, others boil in side.*

> Carmela Tal Baron
> (Twentieth-century Israeli)

The purely primal power that comes from holding and handling eggs at the equinox has been a principal influence on many popular spring ritual practices. Eggs dyed red as the womb were given as gifts at the spring festivals in ancient Egypt, Persia, Greece, and Rome. Greeks still toast each other at Easter dinner by tapping hard-boiled red eggs; the egg that survives the clinking uncracked brings luck for the year. Throughout much of the world, the Spring Equinox has been observed as the start of a new year. New life, new beginning, new year. At Narooz, the Spring Equinox, also celebrated as the New Year, modern Iranians, like their Persian ancestors, exchange red eggs for blessings of luck.

The egg, the complete potential of the creative energy of life contained in a clever package, is used universally as a magical charm. In Ethiopia, ancient Christians outlined the crosses that crowned their churches with ostrich eggs. In China, when a month-old baby was presented for blessing at a temple, an amah entered first, bearing a tray of chickens and eggs. In Europe, eggs were used as a fever cure. An egg was touched to the hot skin of the sufferer and then buried, thus transferring the heat to the earth. In the West Indies, Obeah women use eggs and eggshells to conjure and heal.

Christopher Columbus used egg magic as part of his strategy to gain the support of the Spanish throne for his expedition. He wowed them all at the table one night by challenging the dinner guests to stand an egg on its end. No one was able to accomplish this feat, except, of course, Columbus, who cheated by cracking the eggshell on the bottom to make it flat.

Eggs were used to feed the house spirits at building sites in Borneo, and they are mixed into the foundation of buildings constructed in Bombay. An egg, along with salt and wheat, was offered to a new home in Morocco. Ruins of eighteenth-century buildings in Germany have revealed eggs buried in the foundation, under chimneys, embedded in the mortar of floors beneath doorways, and plastered into the walls of churches. Czech myth has it that two hundred cartfuls of eggs were added to the mortar of Prague's Charles Bridge.

Eggs were the centerpiece of the spring festivals celebrated by the old tribes of northern Europe in honor of Eostre, the Teutonic-Anglo-Saxon goddess of dawn. Brought to Britain by Phoenician traders, she is the same Queen of Heaven celebrated by the Babylonians as Astarte and the Assyrians as Ishtar. On the equinox, eggs were dyed blood-red and rolled in the newly sown soil in order to fertilize the fields. The Moon Hare, sacred animal totem of Eostre, laid additional eggs which were colored and hidden for children to find. This ancient fertility rite, still celebrated each year on the White House Lawn, honors Eostre as the fertile aspect of the dawn. From her name we derive the scientific terminology for the female hormone and reproduction cycle—estrogen and estrus—as well as Easter and the Jewish Queen Esther.

During Purim, the Jewish spring festival, Queen Esther is praised as the heroine who saved her people from a plot of annihilation. But her story predates the biblical Book of Esther. Its roots are in the folktales of those who continued to worship the old goddess, Astarte, Ishtar, calling her Esther. The temple fathers were faced with an enduring, deep-seated reverence for this goddess of spring. Her devotees were determined. Ultimately, the patriarchs accommodated and assimilated the pagan practices of her worshipers into the religion. It is interesting to note that Esther's festival was included as a book of the Bible even though there is not one mention of God in its pages.

Esther's original role as a fertility goddess is evident in the *hamantaschen*, which are the traditional sweet Purim treat. These triangular cakes filled with poppyseed are a flagrant representation of the anatomy of female fertility, filled with eggs, the fruitful seeds of the season. The Christians, too, adapted the symbols, ceremonies, and name of the spring festivities of Ishtar-Esther-Eostre to create Easter. Jesus breaks through the hard, cold coffin shell of death to be reborn every spring. In the resurrection of Christ, we witness the vernal rebirth of the soul.

The egg is as central to the commemoration of the Resurrection at Easter as it once was in the fertile festivals of Eostre. It remains an enduring reminder of the promise of everlasting life. Eggs are still brought, in unbroken continuity, by a special bunny. And, as always, they are still dyed, decorated, rolled, hidden, exchanged, and eaten in spring. The decoration of eggs is the most common Easter custom in the Christian world today. Red eggs in the old style are perhaps the most prevalent cross-culturally, although we in the West are probably more familiar with a pale palette of pastel primavera shades with patterns or polka dots.

The incredibly ornately painted traditional eggs made by Polish and Ukrainian women have developed into the fine folk art of *pysanki*. These women conceive the minutely detailed patterns in deep meditation while sitting alone late at night in the quiet, their families asleep around them. The symbols are ancient, speaking over thousands of years the truths born of earth-based wisdom. They depict the old goddess and her philosophy: Bohynja-Berehynja, the Grand Goddess; Knjahynia, the Princess; Koroleva, the Queen Mother Earth; Stara Baba, Cold Woman. Dots, depending on their configuration, represent stars in heaven, tears, or fixed points that have no beginning and no end. A dot within an enclosing circle stands for the axis of the universe—eternity as seen within an egg.

> *In marble walls as white as milk,*
> *Lined with a skin as soft as silk;*
> *Within a fountain crystal clear,*
> *A golden apple doth appear,*
> *No doors there are to this stronghold,*
> *Yet thieves break in and steal the gold.*

English riddle

The zenith of egg decoration was achieved by Peter Carl Fabergé, the St. Petersburg goldsmith, who created a series of extraordinary, magnificently opulent gold and jewel eggs, all with movable secrets inside, for the last Russian Romanov tsars. In 1880 he produced his first masterpiece, a jeweled egg with a surprise inside, for Alexander III to present to the tsarina at

Easter. Deceptively simple, it looked exactly like a real egg. It was made of gold enameled white and it opened to reveal a golden yolk. Inside the yoke was a hen, and inside the hen was a tiny, diamond-studded imperial crown, which was topped by a ruby egg.

In its natural state, or embellished through myth, ritual, and art, the egg continues to serve as an eloquent symbol for the world. Our universe is as solid as an egg. As durable. Vigorous. Resilient. And that's saying a lot, because an egg is surprisingly strong. It is practically impossible, for instance, for an adult, even Arnold Schwarzenegger, to break an egg simply by squeezing it in one hand. According to *The Guinness Book of Records*, the farthest that a raw hen's egg has been pitched and caught without breaking is 190 feet 10 inches in Auckland, Australia. In a 1970 experiment, a Royal Air Force officer dropped eighteen eggs from a helicopter at 150 feet and only three of them broke!

Our universe, like an egg, is also at the same time quite fragile. Amazingly innocent and very, very vulnerable. The earth, which was once the silver, and the sky, which was once the yolk; the oceans, which were the fluids, and the rivers, which were the veins, are now all suffering from the shortsighted selfishness and stupidity of us poor lost baby chicks. If the world is our egg, we must be the chicken. And as such, we must protect our precious planet egg as fiercely as any mother hen. Treat it with reverence and respect. With unconditional, unmitigated maternal tenderness and careful, creative husbandry.

We can start by standing an egg on its end at the exact equinox moment. Stand an egg on its end and experience that incredible instant of being perfectly in balance. Stand an egg on end and stand with it. Stand in awe of the intricate order, the elegant logic and laws that regulate the workings of our world egg. Stand in support and defense of this virile yet vulnerable universe.

Let us stand on this planet as if we were walking on eggs.

MIDSPRING

By Midspring, the tantrum storms, like the terrible twos of the early part of the season, have stilled. There is a new calmness, a certain confidence, in the air. Nature has taken hold. Once-tentative buds have unfolded and flourished. Flowers, food, and forage are abundant and fragrant. All the vernal newborns, having outgrown generations of teeth, feathers, pelts, and ridiculously expensive sneakers, are now practically exploding with hormones. All-too-ready, set, go, head out on their own. Determined to produce and reproduce.

If Candlemas signals the quickening of life, and the Spring Equinox signifies the time of birth, then May Day, the halfway point of spring, is a puberty rite of passage into adolescence. The season of exuberant youth in all its boundless energy, innocent ardor, and potential creativity. The spring cross-quarter day is the growing time when life seems to shoot up out of the ground and keep on going forever. What we used to call the wonder years.

The whole world is in the throes of a contagious spring fever, a delirious dance of motion and emotion. Life all around is gaudy, giddy, giggly, on an exhilarating carnival ride of heady smells and riotous color. The earth and her species are spread green with the effervescent, aphrodisiac substance of life.

> *Spring is life.*
> *Life is trees.*
> *Trees are oxygen.*
> *They all come together in one place.*
> *Make us breathe and live . . .*
> *Spring is the giving of life.*
>
> Chieu Tran
> Grade 6, I.S. 145

The tree of life, with its roots deep in the earth and its branches reaching upward toward heaven, out toward eternity, is the prime symbol of midspring celebrations in many cultures. Trees have long been worshiped as beneficent spirits of bounty. Trees shade and feed us, supply and sustain us. They breathe life into our lungs. Possessing potent powers of fertility, growth, and longevity, trees are the progenitors of the world family tree.

You can't see the forest for the trees in world mythology.

The Masai people claim their descent to be from an original parent tree. The Mayas of Central America understand themselves to be part of a great celestial ceiba tree. This silk-cotton tree, which stands for all life, is the pole at the center of the earth and serves to hold up the heavens. The Zapotec Tree of Life is two thousand years old, 131 feet tall, and 138 feet in girth. It grows in Santa María del Tule in the Mexican state of Oaxaca. This majestic, stately being large enough to offer shade to five hundred adults, which survived Columbus and survived the conquistadors and survived the Mexican Revolution, is now suffering the consequences of air pollution and a near-depleted groundwater table. The health and prognosis of the Great Tree of Life now hang in precarious balance.

The Koran refers to the cosmos as a tree. Yggdrasil, the World Ash, is the tree goddess of the Scandinavian underworld who overreaches the human abode, touching the sky with her branches. Her roots reach to the very center of the earth where they wind around the sacred wells that impart wisdom. The World Tree is the symbol of all relationship and, as such, is the central philosophical image for the Slavs. The Hebrew goddess Asherah was associated with a sacred tree. The Greek goddess Athena was symbolized by an eternally flourishing olive tree. Helen was worshiped as a tree on the Greek island of Rhodes into the nineteenth century. The Buddha was born under a tree at Lumbini, attained Enlightenment under a tree at Gaya, and entered Nirvana under a tree at Kusinagara.

The Bodhi Tree. The Tree of Life in the Garden of Eden. The Egyptian Tree of Life. The biblical Tree of Knowledge. The Persian Tree Opposed to Harm. The Navaho Tree. The Iroquois Tree of Peace. The Cedar Tree of the Ghost Dance. The Witch Tree of the Ojibwa. The Yoruban Universal Tree of Life. The Taoist Paradise Tree. The Celtic Tree of Paradise. The Germanic World Tree, the Heaven Pillar. The Greek Sacred Pine of Attis. The Tree of Liberty of the French Revolution. The Oaxacan Tule Tree. The Kabbalah Tree. The Cedar of Lebanon. The Christmas Tree.

Charles Darwin explains his theory of natural selection in *Origin of the Species* by way of an exquisitely composed metaphor based on the Tree of Life:

> As buds give rise by growth to fresh buds, and these, if vigorous, branch out and over-top on all sides many a feebler branch, so by generation, I believe it has been with the great Tree of Life, which fills with its dead and broken branches the crust of the earth, and covers the surface with its ever branching and beautiful ramifications.

European Spring Cross-Quarter festivities were held in honor of the trees and their mistresses, the virgin vegetation goddesses. Midspring was celebrated as Floralia by the Romans, Walpurgisnacht by the Teutons, and Beltane by the Celts. Romantic devotions, all, for Flora, Walpurga, and Maia, for whom this month is named. Maia, whose name means "grandmother," "midwife," or "wise one," can be traced back to Maya, the pre-Vedic mistress of perceptual reality who was the virgin mother of the Buddha. The Greek goddess Maia was the virgin mother of Hermes. Blessed Virgin Mary, Mother of God, is patroness of the month of May, which the early church dedicated to her.

> *Spring is purple*
> *jewelry;*
> *flowers on the ground,*
> *green in the forest.*
>
> > Woman's chant,
> > (Ca. Eleventh-century Latin)

On May morning as late as the turn of the twentieth century, young girls would go out in the predawn hours to wash their faces in May dew, which was believed to be fortifying as well as beautifying. At first light, the boys joined them in the forest, and together they brought in the May—small trees, branches, and flowers with which to decorate the village green, streets, and houses. In England, they sang in the May, adding music to their forest procession.

The group of young folk then stripped a tall tree of its branches and set it up in the village square. The top was crowned with a wreath of flowers and sometimes a female figurine as well, clearly a phallus encircled by a yoni. This Maypole was hung with ribbons which were woven around the pole in the course of a grand-right-and-left spiral dance, intertwining the young men and women in the process; bringing them, binding them, ever closer together. In medieval and Tudor Britain, May Day was an important public holiday, sizzling with sexual abandonment. A similar celebration of spring fertility and copulation celebrated in Holland is called Whitsuntide.

Early Midspring rites included the wearing of the green, a symbolic modeling of the earth's verdant new garments, a sign of imitation and identification with the natural world. May Day festivals, which began with great public gaiety, usually ended in orgiastic display of sexual licentiousness. Marriage vows were temporarily forgotten during this honey month. People coupled freely in the woods and fields, fertilizing the soil and each other, sharing a fervent participation in the regenerative magic of the earth.

Why should those branches not remain for ever bare, the earth for ever hard and inhospitable? By what grace did these green hopes and gentle exhalations perpetually recur? He had done nothing to deserve so munificent a resurgence.

Margaret Drabble, *The Needle's Eye*
(Twentieth-century English)

It is no wonder that the puritannical Protestant fathers were deeply offended by the Maypole ceremony with its not-so-subtle sexual connotations and pagan sensibilities. An Act of Parliament in 1644 called for the removal of "Maypoles (a heathenish vanity, generally abused to superstition and wickedness)" and further ordered that "all and singular Maypoles, that are, or shall be erected, shall be taken down and removed by the Constaples, and Church Wardens of the parishes and places where the same be; and that no Maypole shall be hereafter set up, erected, or suffered to be within this Kingdom of England or Dominion of Wales."

Maypoles later regained favor during the Restoration. The last permanent public Maypole was erected in the London Strand in 1661. It took twelve British soldiers under the personal supervision of James II to plant the 134-foot cedar pole in the ground. In 1717 it was removed to Wanstead Park in Essex, where it was used by Sir Isaac Newton as part of the support of the largest telescope in the world. In its new job, the pole, the tree of life, served exactly its original symbolic function—the unification of the earth and the sky.

Like all of the devotional rites dedicated to the earth goddess that they could not repress, May Day was ultimately claimed by the church as its own. In doing so, the veneration of the Maypole/May tree was left completely intact. The tree simply became the cross. Holy Cross Day is observed on May 3, in honor of Empress Helen (the selfsame who was once worshiped as a Goddess Tree). According to the Catholic version, it was she who found the True Cross of Christ under the Temple of Venus(!) in the fourth century A.D. When the Europeans came to the Western Hemisphere, they brought with them a variety of Catholic, Puritan, and peasant May Day practices. These have interfaced with Midspring festivals of indigenous Americans.

Holy Cross Day, as it is celebrated in Mexico and Guatemala, has a distinctly Indian aesthetic of spiritual intimacy. Wooden crosses are erected at places of new beginnings: building sites and roadways and intersections. These are hung like Maypoles with ribbons and decorated with flowers, flags, kerchiefs, even dresses and jewelry. In Chile, the cross is dressed on May 1 and processed through town, where it stops at every home in order to bless it. It is undressed again on May 31.

Aquí anda Santa Cruz
Visitando sus devotos.
Con un cabito de vela
Y un traguito de mosyo.

Here comes the Holy Cross
Visiting its devotees.
With a stump of a candle
and a sip of grape juice.

Traditional Chilean chant

Cruzelacu or Cruz Velakuy is the two-week midspring nature appreciation festival celebrated throughout Latin America beginning on Holy Cross (*cruz*) Day. Hawaii fetes May 1 as Lei Day, an old flower festival stemming from before the missionary invasion of the islands. Thousands of fresh flowers are gathered, strung, and hung from the branches of trees in a springtime ceremony of harmony with nature and appreciation of its creations. In an older, less adulterated expression of the season, the people of the mountains of Guerrero, Mexico, hold a pole dance. The young men lie on the ground, their legs in the air supporting a painted post the size of a telephone pole. Using their feet, they balance, spin, and twirl the painted poles like potent red batons. Proudly, they wave them erect and aloft.

The Brazilian May Day celebration is a marriage between the European Maypole and the West African Universal Tree of Life, which was transported in the slave ships. The same tree spirit was the inspiration for the old African American spiritual "All God's Children Got a Right to the Tree of Life." An especially energetic tree is designated to be the ceremonial stand-in for the Tree of Life. The lower branches are dressed in ribbons. From the top flies the white flag of the Yoruban god of time. An interesting ritual coincident is that in Nepal, half a world away, a tree called the Tree of Life is also hung with white flags at the midpoint of spring.

The Liberty Tree is a common symbol among many North American Indian groups. It represents the freedom of the individual to experience the divinity in nature directly. A single cedar tree called the World Tree stands in the center of the Ghost Dance circle. The Ghost Dance is a ritual born of the healing vision of one individual. In 1888 Wovoka, a Paiute medicine man, created the ceremony of the Ghost Dance to bring together many different Indian nations in a new unity. The Ghost Dance is an assertion of cultural identity, dignity, and spiritual empowerment in the face of degradation, dispersal, and death. The spring midpoint is one of the nine annual Ghost Dances, each held at a gateway time of celestial power.

Jake Swamp, a member of the Mohawk Nation, has carried the Liberty Tree into the 1990s. Inspired by the Great Peacemaker who arose about a thousand years ago during a dark age of war and strife in the history of the Iroquois, he has designed a ceremony for the planting of the Tree of Peace. For several years he has been traveling throughout North America and Europe planting trees with people. The ritual includes the burying of the hatchet. An Indian tomahawk and a part from a nuclear weapon are interred at the foot of the Tree of Peace along with the anger, resentments, ill feelings, and mistrust of the planters.

The closest we come to celebrating an animistic May Day in

twentieth-century America is Arbor Day. Once a year since 1872, on the last weekend in April, schoolchildren, Scouts, and park rangers plant trees in a conscious effort to green the land. It was originally promoted as a holiday by Julius Sterling Morton, a Nebraska settler and conservation advocate, who noticed that cultivating the prairies was resulting in drier soil, which was blowing away. What he saw was the coming of the dust bowl. He instigated the planting of more than a million trees in barren areas during the first year.

Tu Bi-Shevat, the Jewish Arbor Day, is also a relatively new observance, evolved by the Ashkenazim, East European settlers in Palestine, in the seventeenth century. In addition to being the New Year for Trees, Tu Bi-Shevat celebrates the eating of the first ripe fruits of the season. It is ideal to consume four glasses of wine and fifteen different kinds of fruit—for the fifteenth day of the month on which the holiday falls. In China, trees are planted in public places during the Ching Ming, the Bright and Clear Festival. At this time, families also plant trees on the graves of the ancestors. The willow tree, especially, decorates the burial places of the dead, as it has a mystical connection with spring and, hence, rebirth.

A few years ago, I spent Arbor Day planting two hundred white pine seedlings in Prospect Park in Brooklyn with a group of about forty streetwise teenagers from East New York. (This happened to be the same day that Los Angeles was burning over the Rodney King decision.) Along with each tree, we ceremonially planted our prayers and positive intentions for the future, the wishes and hopes and plans that would nourish the planted and the planters alike. One girl remarked that even while she was thrilled to be planting baby trees, she was worried because they wouldn't have a father. I said, "You've heard of Mother Earth." "Yeah." "Well, there is Father Sky." And she perked right up, "Oh yeah, and the wind is the uncle!"

The tree supports and centers our relationship with the earth.

In the tree we can see our own best selves. Standing strong. Our foundation dug in solid rock, seeking the deep source of knowledge. Our stance is solid yet supple. Flexible, our out-ward, upward reach extends, bends always toward the light. We nourish and provide and shelter and heal. We, too, manufacture our sustenance from the sun. We share the very breath of life. We are the tree. The World Family Tree of Humanity. May we grow together to be the Universal Tree of Peace.

Arbol de la esperanza
mantente firme.

Tree of hope
keep firm.

Frida Kahlo
(Twentieth-century Mexican)

THE SUMMER SOLSTICE

Since the Winter Solstice, the shortest day of the year, the sun has been inching its way back into our lives. Rising slightly earlier each morning and, depending on latitude, setting a minute or two later every night, it graces us with light gradually gained. The change is at first imperceptibly slow, but it is steady, and soon the minute-by-minute accumulation of daylight asserts itself in more and more hours of sun.

By the Spring Equinox, the halfway point in the annual solar swing, the days have become about three hours longer in most of the United States. Everywhere on earth, day and night are of equal length at the equinoxes. The constant accretion of light continues for three more months until the Summer Solstice, the longest day of the year. That's about fifteen hours in New York City, twenty-one hours in Fairbanks, Alaska. In Sweden, it is indeed the land of the midnight sun. And at the north pole, the sun doesn't set at all.

Bede, the British monk and scholar who lived around the turn of the eighth century, observed:

> Since Britain lies far north toward the pole, the nights are short in summer, and at midnight it is hard to tell whether the evening twilight still lingers or whether dawn is approaching, since the sun at night passes not far below the earth in its journey round the north back to the east. Consequently the days are long in summer, as are the nights in winter when the sun withdraws into the African regions.

The seasonal ascendance of light and temperature is not—despite popular belief—due to our distance from the sun, but to the degree of directness of its rays. It would be logical, on the face of it, to assume that in the smarmy summer the earth approaches closest to the sun, and that we are farthest away in the cold dark of winter. Wrong! The earth reaches its perihelion, the point on our orbit that brings us closest to the sun, in winter (usually around January 2 or 3); and conversely, during summer (July 5 or so) we attain our aphelion, the farthest reach of our range from the sun.

Though the distance from the sun is greatest in the summer, it is at the Summer Solstice that the sun sits highest in the sky. The steep path of its rays is angled almost vertically overhead. Its energy is aimed arrowlike down on us. The Summer Solstice is the lightest, brightest, most brilliant summit of solar power. The peak, the potent pinnacle. The absolute apex of radiant energy extended toward us from our own shining star.

The Summer Solstice is the height of the glory of the season of the sun. It is at this point that the dark must begin to creep back, bringing cold and death in its wake. The return toward the dark completes the annual solar circuit. The swing shift of sunlight.

For several days before beginning its descent, the sun stands sentinel at dawn. It seems to stand stark still in the sky, which is what "solstice" means—"sun stands still." It stands proud and tall for our total admiration and enthusiastic tribute. As we celebrate the birth of the brand-new sun at the Winter Solstice, we salute its vibrant maturity at the solstice in the summer. We exalt in the season's vital strength—and our own—even as we acknowledge its impending and inevitable loss of virility, fertility, and ultimate demise.

> *How could our eyes see the sun,*
> *unless they are sunlike themselves?*
>
> Johann Wolfgang von Goethe
> (Nineteenth-century German)

The Hopi Summer Solstice ceremony perfectly describes this seasonal shift in terms of a transferral of our spiritual reliance on divine illumination to the realization of our own personal response-ability. Niman Kachina is the "going home" of the kachinas, the guiding spirits of the tribe. Six months earlier at Soyal, the Winter Solstice, the kachinas had come out from their underground digs to join the people. Now they return to the depths of their sacred kivas. Dressed and purified with water and smoke in preparation for their journey, they recede with the light, leaving the people to their own devices. As they depart, they present gifts to the children and bless them. "May you go on your way with happy hearts and grateful thoughts."

In megalithic times, people began to create structures that would enable them to track the course of the sun, the source of life. These solar observatories were specifically designed to give precise determination of the days of the solstices, the two days, opposite in the year, that are the times of greatest extreme. It was necessary to calculate the longest summer day, since it serves as a signal light, a warning sign for changes in light and weather to come. If the solstice is observed, preparation can be made for survival of the approaching cold.

Indigenous Europeans, predating the Druids, who are usually associated with them, built many such sun shrines. Stonehenge, the most famous standing stone circle, has its main axis in perfect alignment with the Summer Solstice sunrise. Strikingly similar monuments to the movements of the heavens were built by the ancestors of the tribes of the Great Plains of the northern United States and Canada. These sunburstlike designs—wheels with twenty-eight spokes—were laid out in rock on the great grasslands. They, too, were positioned in exact orientation to the solstice sunrise. There are more than fifty known medicine wheels, some dating back 2,500 years.

The Chumash Indians of California left a legacy of caves which they converted into solstice observatories. These "Houses of the Sun" feature apertures cut into the walls or ceilings which—only at the exact sunrise moment—allow a beam of light to enter the dark cave and shine on the sacred rock art inside. The Aztecs of Mexico, the Mesoamerican Mayas, the Incas of Peru, the Chinese, and the Egyptians all left architectural testimony to their astronomical sophistication and solstice supplication. Without written records, it is unclear precisely what went on in and around these constructions, except, presumably, sky viewing.

The very sighting of the Summer Solstice sunrise is ceremony in its simplest and purest form. Observance = observance. The noting itself is a greeting, a simple salutation to the strongest sun. Greeks would kiss their hand and salute the sun with it. Ritual observation of such a Celestially Auspicious Occasion allows one to enter into a personal, physical partnership with the powers of nature. Here, one is privy to the powerful reality of a participatory universe. The sunrise seen is experienced as a mutual endeavor.

> *There!*
> *There!*
> *Beautiful white-rising has dawned*
> *Beautiful yellow-rising has dawned*
> *There!*
> *There!*

> Hopi song

Throughout Europe, Catholic Canada, and Central and South America, it is still popular to stay awake this shortest night of the year to watch the solstice sunrise. To stand witness to the wonder. To this day, the people of the Taos Pueblo race up the mountain to welcome the rising solstice sun. To meet it halfway, as it were. For them, it is a form of reciprocation. A returning, in much gratitude, of some life-giving energy to its original source. An allegorical passing of the life force torch. Light is not lost lightly. Light equals life for all living things. The grim prospects of life in the dark prod one to take action. To enlist in the service of the sun, the solar cheering section. The stars need stirring, the atmosphere, a charge. This is the task at hand if all is not to be lost. Sympathetic magic is called for to fan the floundering flames of *el sol*.

In pagan Europe and North Africa, people sent burning wooden hoops and wheels woven of straw rolling down steep hills to illustrate the retreat of the sun, spinning, turning, traveling away. These wheels descend from a much older solar symbol, the chariot. The Norse *Eddas* tell of the goddess Sol, Sul, Sulis, driving the chariot of the sun. Ancient Buddhist texts speak of the sun chariot as the Great Vehicle or the Chariot of Fire. The ancient Greeks pictured the Sun carried across the daytime sky in a golden chariot. On the Summer Solstice, the priests of the Sun and Poseidon along with the priestess of Athena processed in front of the Acropolis with gift offerings of fruit and libations of honeycombs. Wine was not served because it would make the Sun tipsy and he had to drive.

The actual lighting of bonfires is by far the most prevalent—practically universal—practice for celebrations of the solstice. What more fitting offering could be made in the aid of the failing mother of all light? It is the ultimate act of flattery by imitation. The primal sacrament of obeisance to the first flame of the firmament. A symbolic feeding of restorative fresh strength to the sun. And at the same time, certainly, the light and heat of the fire serve to soothe and affirm that, though departing, the sun will surely return.

In ancient Egypt, the Summer Solstice was celebrated by the Burning of the Lamps at Sais in honor of Isis, Queen of Heaven. In Rome, the day was dedicated to Vesta, known as Hestia in Greece. The Vestal Virgins, her oracular priestesses, were the guardians of the public hearth and altar. On this day the perpetual fire representing the mystical heart of the empire was extinguished, rekindled, and blessed.

> *Osiris!*
> *Osiris!*
> *when the Ra-Disc glides onward in the Sun-boat*
> *flamespurts spew off the prow*
> *O may I catch thy spurts o brother*

> *as the shrieking human*
>   *catches the sun!*

>> Incantation by Isis
>> for the revival of the dead Osiris

People across the European continent and their New World colonies built great bonfires on the solstice. They danced around them the whole night long in a joyful, spirited vigil. They danced in great circles, winding to assist the sun on its celestial course. They leaped through the flames and drove their animals through them to be empowered and purified by the heat, the smoke. They waved torches in the air, passed them over crop and stock, and sent them out to sea. Blessings, all, of the sun's supreme power.

Many of these practices have been maintained until quite recently. The solstice is celebrated throughout the Catholic world as the Nativity of St. John the Baptist and is, for the most part, observed in the same manner as the fire festivals of old. The prevalence of solstice fire festivals in Arab lands such as Morocco and Algeria is particularly interesting because the solstice is a solar milestone, and the Islamic calendar, which is completely lunar, does not note holidays that occur at fixed solar points of the year. These summer rituals are relics of a remembered, far older faith when their forebears worshiped the bold sun as the Great Mother Atthar or Al-llat.

In the Western Hemisphere, too, fires are lit and danced around, firebrands shot into the air, and fragrant herbs burned and offered as cleansing smoke. The Dakota people of North Dakota have held a Sun Dance at the solstice since 1876, when ten thousand people joined in this ritual with their spiritual leader, Crazy Horse. Participants offer their own bodies to the sun, the glorious manifestation of Wakan-Tanka, the all-embracing great and sacred spirit. "As you know the moon comes and goes, but *annpetu wi*, the sun, lives on forever; it is the source of light, and because of this it is Wakan-Tanka," said Black Elk in reference to the Sun Dance.

People promise to dance in order to fulfill vows made at times of deep stress or danger, famine or battle. They dance for up to four days without food or water, facing the sun, suspended from the pole in the center of the circle by cords threaded through their skin. Like any good mother, they sacrifice their own flesh, thirst, and hunger. Their incredible endurance. Their pain and their power to transcend pain. All so that the nation, the entire world, shall thrive.

According to Russell Means, a leader of the American Indian Movement and survivor of the armed occupation at Wounded Knee in 1973 on the site of the Pine Ridge Reservation massacre of 1890, during the Sun Dance "we want to get in touch with the female, so we create purification ceremonies for boys and men to bring us to an understanding of what it is like to give birth. . . . During those four days and nights we do not eat or drink water so we can try to begin to understand the suffering of pregnancy. . . . On the fourth day we pierce our chests, maybe even our backs, to understand the pain and the giving of flesh and blood the woman goes through."

The buffalo is a significant symbol of the Sun Dance. Life depends on the buffalo. The buffalo depends on the grass. The grass depends on the sun. And, especially at the Summer Solstice, the sun depends on us. The same conceptual collaboration exists in the St. John's bonfire celebrations and those of Islamic North Africa. There is the same correlation between the sun and the harvest, the fires and the future. They are united as if by cosmic umbilical cord. The higher the flames, the taller the grain.

These fiery fetes focus us on the fertile power of the sun and on the fecundity of the plants and animals that feed us. If the sun is at its zenith in the sky, so, too, is nature here on earth at the summit of its sumptuousness. "As above, so below," the Talmud tells us. The sap has risen. The plants are in their prime. First fruits and flowers, grasses and game, offer themselves for the taking. Trees are resplendent in their rich garments of verdure. The landscape is lush with life.

In addition, these sun festivals are a celebration of our own part in the propagation of life. Like the sun and the sap, the libido also rises. Out of its basket it surges, the charmed serpentine call of the wild. No sissy spring fever, this. But full-fledged, full-bodied, full of pluck, magenta plush lust. Robust. Randy, willing, and able. The season surging in their pulse, people, too, are quite ripe by the solstice. Plump and juicy, and ready to pick.

For the members of the Voodoo cults of New Orleans, St. John's Day was the most important holiday of the year. The main ceremony was a ritual dance called the *calinda*, which was performed by the Voodoo Queen, Mam'zelle Marie la Veau, around a fire to the frenzied beat of conga drums and gourds. The dancers would twist and turn, gyrate and shake. Twirl and swirl in sinuous, tantalizing imitation of the sacred African serpent. Crowds of whites and Creoles would gather around the sizzling plaza, Congo Square, to fuel the heat of their own horny loins.

> *Midsummer night is not long,*
> *But it sets many cradles rocking.*

> Swedish proverb

The Summer Solstice has long been a lovers' holiday. Here is the power that can refuel the universe. Over the ages, customs and myths have arisen to encourage—to ritualize—a summer mating season in order to ensure a successful procreation. Pro-life means more than having children. It means having a way of keeping them alive. If people coupled in the spring when they first start feeling the fever, the baby would be born at the beginning of winter. Just in time for the start of the long months of cold and hunger. It would be like shooting craps with the infant mortality rate.

Ovid relates an oracle he received from the priestess of Jupiter pertaining to the impending marriage of his daughter. She counseled him to have her wait "until the Ides of June." "There is no luck for brides and their husbands until the sweepings from the Temple of Vesta have been carried down to the sea by the yellow Tiber." June 15 was Vestalia, the Roman solstice celebration when the altars to Vesta were renewed. The Festival of New Fire.

On the Summer Solstice, aroused young girls in many places practice divination to determine the identity of their own true love. Charms are placed in the fire, over the heart, and under the pillow. As they jump over the fire in Portugal, they sing:

> *In praise of St. John—*
> *May he give health to my heart.*
> *St. John comes and St. John goes;*
> *Mother, marry me off soon!*

In the Greek countryside, one can still see St. John's wedding processions made up of masquerading children. The miniature bride and groom, properly veiled and suited, are preceded by a young boy baring a rod and followed by a bevy of tiny, twittering ladies-in-waiting. Shakespeare's *A Midsummer Night's Dream* is a sweet one of rightfully requited love, a tour de forest in which the convoluted courtships of two pairs of lovers come to a happily-ever-after ending.

June weddings are still very much in style. But the rest—the worshipful awe of nature, the respect, the reverence—has all disappeared. The universal scenario has shifted, and the world will never be the same. We wanted to rise above, to regiment, to rape, to rule, Mother Nature. And for several thousand years, we have. We tried to fix what wasn't broken, and we've wreaked havoc with the beautiful balance.

And so the sun, the center of cosmic energy, has become something to stay out of. The fires burn out of control. The deserts are spreading. The shorelines are shrinking. Our wholesome soil washes out to sea. People die daily from too little food, and others from too much. There are way too many babies being born, and way too many dying.

I have a proposal to make. And I'm down on one knee to do it. This solstice, shall we engage in holy wedlock with the world? Shall we pledge our troth to the earth, to the sun, to all of nature and each other? Shall we promise to have and to hold? To love and to honor, to respect and protect, our most beauteous and beloved planet? Shall we take her as our cherished bride and stride off into a secure future of fond and careful husbandry?

MIDSUMMER

The halfway point of summer is like a well-seasoned woman. The galloping growth of spring and sweet blush of early summer have slowed and faded in her sweltering heat. She's slower now, stronger and surer. She's salty and sultry and a little bit dusty. She bears the fruits of her own labors, and she wears them well. By midsummer, Dame Nature has grown tired of her wardrobe with its dizzy palette of vibrant greens, vivid pinks, randy reds, and profusions of pretty pastels. She now prefers the warmer, deeper, richer tones more flattering to her present station.

> Age is not all decay: it is the ripening, the swelling, of the fresh life within, that withers and bursts the husks.
>
> George MacDonald
> (Nineteenth-century Scottish)

The summer cross-quarter day marks the ripening season. Trees and vines, stems and stalks, are hung heavy with the abundance of the earth. Although animals, birds, and fish now are easy targets for hunters, the growth of grain holds the strongest significance for the midsummer season. Grain, the staple, the sustenance, the stuff, the staff of life.

From grain comes bread. Bread making is one of the oldest human arts. Calcified remains of cakes made from coarsely ground grain which date back to the Stone Age have been found in Swiss lake dwellings at Wangen and Robenhausen. Perhaps the first form of bread was prepared from crushed acorns and beechnuts, a recipe still used in many Native North American cuisines.

The idea for bread making is an extremely clever and sophisticated one involving an almost magical alchemical conversion of matter in consort with the elemental forces of nature. Consider the process: In fields of wildflowers tall grasses grow. First green, then gold, they yield tiny compact kernels which, stripped of their papery casings, pounded, and ground into powder, can be mixed with water and baked by fire to produce bread.

The development of clay pots, and the kilns in which they were fired, suggested innovative ways of preparing grain for consumption, revolutionizing the dietary habits of the vast majority of people worldwide. Bread in its endless unleavened varieties—flat bread, fry bread, oatcake, johnnycake, tortilla, pita, paratha, pappadam, naan, ingera, matzoh, blini—as well as other cereal stuffs—porridge, pozole, polenta, pone, pilaf, pasta, tsampa, tamale, congee, kasha, couscous, gruel, grits, mush—soon replaced animal flesh as the staff of life. This carbohydrate-concentrated fare was augmented with greens, gathered and grown, and seasoned with only the occasional portion of a feast meat offering.

Basic bread has long been thought to be the one essential food, along with water, for survival. The sustenance of prisoners and penitents, sinners and saints, alike. Bread has come, in fact, to symbolize food itself. Its vital importance is clear in such common expressions as "earning one's bread," "taking the bread out of somebody's mouth," "knowing which side one's bread is buttered on," and "thank you for our daily bread." In English slang, "bread" equals money, another essential commodity. "Having a bun in the oven" is a marvelous metaphor for pregnancy, the nurturance of life baked in the warm and nurturing womb of Mother Nature.

> Under the ashes which unmake themselves like a bed, watch the round loaves and the square loaves puff up.
> Feel their deep animal heat and the elusive heart perfectly centered like a captive bird.
>
> Anne Hébert
> (Twentieth-century Canadian)

Considering this miracle of transformation, it is no wonder that bread was held to have curative and magical powers. In Belgium, bread was placed in the cradle to protect the baby from illness or harm. In Egypt, it was considered a cure for indigestion. In Morocco, it was a specific against stammering. And in certain communities of the United States, bread, when placed with coffee under a house, was said to keep away the ghosts. St. Hildegard, abbess of the Bingen convent in the twelfth century, prescribed bread as a cure for loss of mind that had been caused by a magic spell. In order to be efficacious, the loaf first had to be inscribed, "May God, who cast away all precious stones from the devil . . . cast away from thee all phantoms and all magic spells, and free thee from the pain of madness."

New houses were blessed, friendships sealed, oaths taken, agreements consecrated, and contracts made by eating bread and salt. The sharing of bread is also associated with peace and the resolving of differences. Eating a meal together, a sacramental and physical union of communality, is the most prevalent way in which people admit a stranger into a kindred relationship. Engaging in armed conflict is almost unthinkable if the parties have eaten together. The Egyptian hieroglyphic for peace, rendered *hotep*, is a loaf of bread resting on a reed mat.

English girls appealed to the three goddesses of fate by passing bread crumbs three times through a wedding ring, in order to be rewarded with a glimpse of their future husbands. Bread has been used as an aphrodisiac by French brides who aroused the passion of their new husbands by sharing with them a sweet baked loaf called "the bride's pasty," the forerunner of our wedding cake. On the flip side, abused wives would visit the shrine of St. Wilgefortis in St. Paul's Cathedral in London with offerings of pecks of cut grain and prayers that their husbands, who were, perhaps, too aroused and rowdy, might drop dead soon. Apparently, their pleas were heard, because St. Wilgefortis gained the nickname St. Uncumber.

The reaping of the first ripened grain was great cause for celebration in honor of the Great Grain Mother who feeds us all. She has been known by many names: Astarte, Ashoreth, Isis, Demeter, Ceres, Op, Terre Mater, Tailltiu, Chicomecóatl, Green Corn Girl, Blue Corn Girl, Mother Quescapenek. The

English word "lady" is derived from the Old English *hlaf-dige*. The root word, *hlaf*, means "loaf," and *dige* means "kneader." Used together, they have the connotation of woman, lady of the house, as provider, "giver of daily bread."

> *The golden grain piles high in the yard.*
> *Round, round wheat, better than pomegranate seeds.*
> *Bite it with your teeth, it goes "go-pou!"*
> *The first pile of wheat is really lovely.*
> *After we have dried it in the sun,*
> *And cleaned it,*
> *We will turn it into the public share.*

> Li Chü, "Harvesting Wheat
> for the (Collective) Public Share"
> (Twentieth-century Chinese)

It becomes clear in the hunt and in the harvest that some things must die so that others may live. And so the taking of life, animal and vegetable, becomes a sacrificial act surrounded with much awe and thanks and praise. Life is never to be taken lightly.

In gratitude, people made offerings of the first harvested ears of corn, corn being the generic term for a multitude of grains: wheat, barley, millet, oats, rice, rye, spelt, Quinoa, buckwheat, sorghum, as well as what we know as maize or Indian corn. Fresh-cut sheaves were bundled and braided, decorated with ribbons and flowers, and placed at the altars of the Grain Mother. Considered very potent, the first corn was also held to be an effective love charm, symbolizing, as it did, fertility, prosperity, and growth. Throwing rice at the bride and groom after a wedding is a relic of this belief.

In pagan Europe, the first sheaves at midsummer and the last sheaves at the autumn harvest were twisted and shaped into corn dollies, which were the embodiment of the harvest. She was called Corn Mother, Harvest Mother, Mother Sheaf, Old Woman, Queen, and was honored in different ways in different places. She was left in the fields. She was taken to dances. She was promenaded through the town. She was kept for good luck for one year. She was ceremonially cremated on a funeral pyre to be resurrected in the sowing of the spring seeds. Whatever the occasion, she was always well dressed.

Bread, too, was traditionally offered. Teutonic women who had once made offerings of their own hair to the goddess developed the braided loaves that are popular in Germany. These were called *Berchisbrod*, or bread offered to the goddess Berchta. German Jews called the braided Sabbath challah *Berches*. A Swedish custom is to bake a bread from the last sheaf of grain into the shape of a young girl. This recalls a much earlier sacrifice to the Great God/dess of the Fields of Grain. According to the Hindu Satapatha Brahmana, "In the beginning, the sacrifice most acceptable to the gods was man." In later times, "for the man a horse was substituted, then an ox, then a sheep, then a goat, until at length it was found that the gods were most pleased with the offerings of rice and barley."

Symbol for life that it was, bread represented and was revered as the body of the deity whose gift it was. The Egyptians were among the first to eat their god in the form of bread. Wheat was cultivated on the mummy case of Osiris and baked into communion cakes. By eating them, worshipers could partake of the divinity of the god and, like him, become immortal. The flesh of Adonis and Dionysus was likewise consumed as wheaten cakes. And the blood of Dionysus as well as that of Bacchas was drunk as wine. In Aztec Mexico, effigies of the god Huitzilopochtli were molded from dough made of roasted maize with beet seeds and honey twice a year in May and December. These were broken into pieces and shared by his devotees.

The Catholic ritual of the Eucharist, the offering of the body of Christ to his father, God, is a direct descendant of this ancient pagan practice. The official church doctrine of transubstantiation—that the bread and wine are the actual, literal body and blood of Jesus—calls for absolute faith in the impossible. This concept created quite a controversy, and by the Middle Ages it drew widespread dissent from within the ranks of the church. Eventually, this resulted in the formation of the first Protestant churches. Voltaire's summation of the transubstantiation quarrels was, "Catholics eat God but not bread; Calvinists eat bread but not God; and the Lutherans eat both."

Most nourishing of all bread, the Holy Host has been credited with being able to put out fires, fertilize fields, stimulate a hive's honey production, keep caterpillars out of the vegetable garden, cure sick pigs, and gain freedom for incarcerated prisoners. It got so that people abstained from swallowing the Host that the priest placed in their hand at Mass, so that they could horde it for a rainy day. Determined to keep the Host in the province of the church and not the service of the devil, priests began dispensing the Host directly onto their congregants' tongues.

The Summer Cross-Quarter Day was celebrated by the Saxons as Hlaf Mass, Feast of Bread, and by the Celts as Lughnasadh, Commemoration of Lugh. Lugh was the grain god, son of Mother Earth. Every August he was sacrificed with the reaping of the corn only to be born again in the new shoots of spring exactly as the Egyptian Osiris had been. At the moment of death, according to Egyptian scriptures, a person is also a kernel of grain, "which falls into the earth in order to draw from her bosom a new life." Loaf Mass and Lugh Mass evolved into Lammas, the Druid corn feast, one of the eight cornerstone festivals around which their year revolved. When the church adopted, co-opted, Lammas, it was referred to as Lamb's Mass in commemoration of St. Peter in Chains, and the practice of the offering of the first fruits on the altar remained exactly the same.

Now Lammas comes in
Our harvest begins.
We have now to endeavor to get the corn in.
We reap and we mow,
And stoutly we blow
And cut down the corn that sweetly did grow.

Traditional English song

All of these celebrations of the first corn were observed on August 1. Named for Juno Augusta of Rome, August was particularly sacred to the Goddess Who Gives All Life and Feeds It, Too. It was considered for this reason an especially propitious time to be born. To this day, when a Scot says that someone was born in August, it is a compliment in praise of skilled accomplishment, with absolutely no bearing on the person's actual birthday.

The midsummer cross-quarter day is the only one of the four that is not still actively celebrated in our contemporary culture. Midsummer is celebrated in Europe, but there it refers to June 21, the first day of summer and not the middle at all. Shakespeare's *A Midsummer Night's Dream* actually takes place on the Summer Solstice. The only living vestige of Lammas in the United States is a rural holiday called Second Planting. But unless you read the *Farmer's Almanac* or belong to the Grange or 4-H Clubs, you would have no reason to hear about it. It is celebrated exactly as midsummer has always been celebrated. The first grain is harvested, threshed, milled, baked into bread and cake, and brewed into beer, then shared in community. After a night of feasting and dancing, work starts again at first light, planting the second crop of summer wheat, which will mature by the fall harvest.

How can we, separated from the agricultural process by city and century, appreciate the atmosphere of the season that surrounds us but that we cannot see? What is the Goddess of Grain to us of the supermarket? The patisserie?

Well, we can behave, as they say, as if we were born in August. We can, in fact, become august—wise and generous and gloriously noble, each in our own chosen path. We can hone our skills as the tenders of Mother Earth. We can hoe our row. We can carry our load. We can break bread together. We can feed the hungry.

We reap what we sow.

THE AUTUMN EQUINOX

Autumn ushers in the dark season. The season of diminished light. From now until the Vernal Equinox, six months hence, the nights are longer than the days. Shade and chill prevail. The year, the season, the sun, are slowing down, growing cold, getting old. The insidious forces of death sweep in and overshadow the vibrant life source. The air and land, once alive with teeming species, are becoming empty and mute.

Fall is like being sixty. Having weathered the cycles, the rainbows and the storms, the trials and the troubles, the struggles, the teachings of a full life, it is now the season to reap what you have sown. If you planted your seeds in the spring and tended them well—watered and weeded, pruned and staked, mulched and sprayed, propitiated and prayed; and if the weather was willing—enough, but not too much, sun, wind, and rain; and if you were lucky—favored by the powers-that-be in the universe—come autumn it is prime time to harvest your crop. This is the future you have been saving for. In fall, you cash in and collect the fruits of your love and long labor.

> *Harvest-home, harvest-home.*
> *We have ploughed, we have sowed,*
> *We have reaped, we have mowed,*
> *We have brought home every load,*
> *Hip, hip, hip, harvest-home!*

Traditional English harvest song

Throughout world mythology, the goddess of the good ground, the grain, the autumn harvest, has been appropriately portrayed as a knowledgeable woman of the world, mistress of all earthly domains. A matriarch. She is the Great Mother who sustains all her species. She was known as Astarte, Ishtar by the ancient Semites, Semele by Phrygians, Isis in Egypt, Demeter in Greece, and Ceres in Rome. She is Tari Pennu to the Bengalis, Old Woman Who Never Dies to the Mandans, and Mother Quescapenek to the Salish. To the Aztecs, she is Chicomecóatl, and the Huichols call her Our Mother Dove Girl, Mother of Maize.

Autumn age provides perspective. Here is the potential to ripen to a healthy, golden perfection before the stalk of life is scythed. To propagate the plentiful seeds of genes, of experience, of heritage, of the accumulated wisdom of the generations grown patiently over time. These are the seeds of survival. In the fall of their lives when plants are past their prime, as their last productive act and in a grand-finale flurry of display, they go to seed. They issue forth from themselves the fertile means to assure a continuous succession.

> *Our mother of the growing fields,*
> *our mother of the streams, will have pity upon us.*
> *For to whom do we belong?*
> *Whose seeds are we?*
> *To our mother alone do we belong.*

Cágaba tribe, Venezuela

The parent plants scatter these precious seeds to the four directions. They send them out on the winds and over the waters, and arrange for them to be delivered in the fur of animal couriers and dispersed from the air by birds and bats. Given over to the grain harvesters of many species. It is imperative that these wild and domestic seeds find their way back into the earth womb to germinate and grow again. This accomplished, their lives complete, their genetic deed done, they die. Their decomposing leaves and stalks serve to cover the embryonic seed asleep in the cold ground. Even in death, they serve to nourish new life.

Autumn, then, is inexorably associated with ripe maturity, harvest, and death, as well as the implicit understanding of an eventual rebirth; the offer of resurrection. Just as the dying sun is sure to return, so, too, will the seeds buried deep in the dark begin to sprout come springtime. This potent promise of prospective plenitude sustains us through the empty-stomach months.

While the earth herself is seen as the fertile mother from whom all life has issued, her aspect as the spirit of the grain is celebrated in many cultures as Mother Earth's child. This young one represents next year's crop curled like a fetus within the seeds of this year's harvest. Typically, she is the daughter, the harvest maiden, the corn virgin, although in Aztec Mexico and Egypt, the grain spirit was her son. Also Aztec was Xilonen, Goddess of New Corn. The Cherokees called her Green Corn Girl. To the Prussians, she was the Corn Baby, to the Malays, the Rice Baby. In parts of India, the harvest maiden is Guari, and she is represented by both an unmarried girl and a bunch of balsam plants.

The archetypal grain mother/daughter pair is personified in Greek mythology as Demeter and Persephone, also known as Kore, the virgin goddess. They illustrate two aspects, the crone and the maiden, of the same divine mother spirit. Demeter is this year's ripe crop, and Persephone the seed corn taken from the parent. Like the seed sown in autumn, she symbolically descends into the underworld, torn from the breast of her mourning mother. And, again like the seed, she reappears, reborn, in the spring.

The harvest is experienced at once as a drama of death and a festival of life. In the fall, we commemorate the seasonal demise of the light as well as the plants that provide us sustenance. Even as we glory in the great yield, the reward of our diligence, we mourn the death of the deity residing in the grain, killed by the cutting of the crops. At harvest, we honor s/he who died so that we might continue to live.

> *The Medicine songs,*
> *The songs of magic healing;*
> *The medicine herbs by the water borders,*
> *They will miss me;*
> *The basket willow,*
> *It will miss me;*

All the wisdom of women,
It will miss me.

Alas, that I should die,
Who know so much.

Southern Shoshone

Despite the clear and rational necessity, there is considerable and understandable reluctance to scythe the last sheaf of grain. For here lives the Great Grain Mother and her child—she who has always fed us, to whom we owe our existence. Can we slash her body with a sickle? Can we allow her to be tread upon and trampled on the threshing floor? Can we cook and eat her seed and feed her broken corpse to the animals?

In ancient Egypt, the reapers beat their breasts and cried aloud as they worked. Their mournful laments invoked Isis, the goddess who introduced corn, grain, to her faithful. These doleful dirges at the death of the grain are called *maneros*, in reference to the phrase "Come to thy house," a funeral chant that appears in the Book of the Dead and other Egyptian scriptures. Plaintive harvest songs were sung throughout western Asia as well. In Phoenicia, they moaned strains of "Woe to us!" as they scythed the sheaves.

According to the Cherokees, corn sprang from the blood of an old woman who was murdered by her own wayward sons. Once the last corn was gathered, the harvesters stood at the four corners of the field and wept and wailed, lamenting the bloody death of Selu, the Old Woman of the Corn. After the ingathering, special care was taken to make sure the path from the fields to the village was kept clear in order to encourage Old Woman Maize to stay home and not wander about.

A sorrowful harvest ceremony is celebrated by the women farmers of the Nandi people of East Africa. When the eleusine grain is ripe, they go into the fields with their daughters, light a fire of prescribed plants, and then pluck some of the seeds. Each mother and girl puts one in her necklace, then after chewing another one, she rubs it on her forehead, throat, and breast. With great sadness, they cut the grain and return home with basketfuls to dry. In India today, people perform related elaborate rites for bringing the soul of the rice from the fields to the barn.

> *Autumn, a time to harvest*
> *When vegetables give up their lives,*
> *For the lives of you, people.*
> *Oh, people, don't be sorry*
> *Death is part of life,*
> *One day you will die, too.*

Shefali Parikh
Grade 5, P.S. 150

A harvest custom of the Arabs of Moab clearly embodies the concept of an old and dying corn spirit. When the harvest is all but complete, the last remaining wheat is gathered together and bound before it is cut. A grave-shaped hole is dug and the bundle buried with all due ceremony for the dead. A stone is placed upright at the head and at the foot exactly as in a human funeral. The sheik then intones, "The old man is dead." The people pray, "May Allah bring us back the wheat of the dead."

One can easily imagine that the earth goddess has offered up her life in the form of the fruits of the land. In doing so, she commits the supreme sacrifice. She expends all her generative energy. It is as if Mother Nature in autumn is in the midst of her menopause, her sacred seed spent. In grateful response, she is fed fresh blood to replenish her powers of procreation.

As late as the nineteenth century, the Kandhs of Bengal sacrificed a person for the earth goddess, Tari Pennu, in order to ensure healthy crops and immunity from disease. Blood was especially important in the cultivation of turmeric, which needed it to develop its rich, red color. The Uraons of Chota Nagpur in northeastern India offered human sacrifices to Anna Kuari, who blesses the harvest. And the Lhota Nagas of Brahmapootra severed the heads, hands, and feet of their victims and planted them in the fields for fertilizer.

Aztec hymns tell us that Tonacacihuatl, Our Lady of Substance, was once the goddess of the hunt, blood, and night, but as the people grew to depend more on agriculture, she evolved into the earth goddess. The son of her fertility was the corn, which was identical with the obsidian knife, her symbol. These were the phallic representations of Xipe, the young god identified with the corn and the sunlight, both of which grew up and increased to maturity from the depths of the dark earth.

> In the eighth month they slew a woman in honor of the goddess of tender maize and eight days before this all men and women young and old feasted and danced. . . .
>
> Aztec

Here, too, fertility, death, and sacrifice are connected. The husking of the corn is perceived as the same act as the tearing out of a sacrificial victim's heart, both accomplished with the obsidian blade. At the celebration of the broom harvest of the Earth Mother, first an older woman and then a young girl were beheaded and their blood spread on fruit, seeds, and grain to guarantee abundance.

At the Autumn Equinox purification feast of the ancient Incas of Peru, families first bathed and then anointed their bodies with a substance called *zancus*, which was made from grain mixed with human blood. It was also applied to the thresholds of their homes as a protective charm. The Indians of Guayaquil, Ecuador, used to sow their fields with blood and human hearts to assure the harvest. And the Bagobos of Mindanao in the Philippines offered human sacrifices when sowing the rice fields. The Bontoks and the Apoyaos of the interior of Luzon, also in the Philippines, hunted human heads to be offered at both planting and harvest times.

The sacrificial victim was meant to be an embodiment of the grain and was chosen because of some obvious resemblance to it. For example, the Aztecs would kill young victims to represent young corn and mature ones to stand for the ripe. The Marimos of Africa would choose a short, fat man, round as a seed. The Skidi Pawnees of North America would fatten their female victim before the kill to assure an abundant crop of plump corn.

The identification of the victim with the grain is also evident in the means of execution. A West African queen used to have a man and a woman killed with the implements of cultivation, hoes and spades, and then buried with the seed in the soil. One of the sacrificial practices of the Aztecs was to kill the victim by grinding her or him, like the maize, between two millstones.

> *Sprout seeds for me, I want them growing*
> *in the yellow chalk of my bones.*
>
> Juana de Ibarbourou
> (Twentieth-century Uruguayan)

With the martyred death of the sacrificial victim, the fertile blood seed, like the grain, brings life anew to the world. And, thus, the circle is complete. The death of the old grain, the old sun, the old season, feeds the continuing life of the people. The death of a representative person is then offered in obeisance as repayment of the ultimate debt of life. Death feeds life feeds death. The enduring saga of the eternal cycle of survival.

And, because the struggle is so strong, so long, those who thrive, like the grain, to the ripe age of maturity rate our utmost admiration. The old ones. The autumn ones. The ancestors. The crones. The matriarchs and patriarchs. The ones who remember. The ones who know. The ones who show and tell; the ones who teach. The ones who pass the past and fuel the future. The ones who have gone to seed.

What a glorious deed, indeed! To bring forth from one's self the fertile possibility of continuity! To embed the stuff of one's self in the soil and grow there! Only a culture such as ours, critically out of touch and at emotional odds, divorced and dangerously disassociated from the divine life and death cycle of reality, could possibly consider "going to seed" a derogatory description of old age.

> *Our old women gods, we ask you!*
> *Our old women gods, we ask you!*
> *Then give us long life together,*
> *May we live until our frosted hair*
> *Is white; may we live till then*
> *This life that now we know!*
>
> Tewa prayer for long life

MIDFALL

Everything has a shadow. Night is the shadow of day. Winter is the shadow of summer. Sickness is the shadow of health. Old age, the shadow of youth. And death is the shadow of life. A world without shadows would appear very flat and lifeless, indeed. If it were not for the shadows, we could not appreciate the light. It is the contrast that illuminates.

By the halfway point of fall we are surrounded by an ambient prescience of impending death. Death and decline. Death and disappearance. The sun seems to be dying as we approach the Winter Solstice six weeks away. Our world is steeped in deep shadows, the light decreases daily, dimming toward the shortest, darkest day of the year. And the year itself is reaching the end; drawing to a close. Another cycle completing its course.

We pull ourselves close; cover up and snuggle down. In the season full of shadows we are inclined to explore the darkness inside of us. What we discover there, if we are willing to recognize it, is the inevitability of our own demise. Everything does, after all, die, doesn't it?

> *I live but I cannot live forever.*
> *Only the great earth lives forever.*
> *The great sun is the only living thing.*
>
> "Crazy-Dog Society Song"
> Kiowa

How could we contemplate life without death? What could it ever mean? Death is a part of life. The life cycle includes death, as light includes the shadows, as the day includes the night. The shadow of death offers us the insight to comprehend the vast yet vulnerable continuum of life. Understanding this, we are able to begin to imagine our own place in the eternal procession of the ages. We are reminded of all those who have preceded us and all those who will follow. Successions of generations. Like the fruit of a tree, the generations bud, bloom, ripen, then fall, each in its own turn. And the death of each nurtures and informs the life of the next. Linking the living and dead together in one unbroken chain.

The Autumn Cross-Quarter Day, when all of nature seems to be dying, has long been observed as a feast of the dead in the cultures of the Northern Hemisphere. The occasion at once mourns and rejoices the death of the bounty of the land. In hunting cultures, the corpses of the slain animals were commonly wined and dined in style, in great ceremony as befits a hero. A roast, as it were. Meat was placed in the mouth of the dead beast so that its spirit would gossip about how hospitable these people were. This, it was hoped, would encourage other animals to approach them to be killed, too.

The celebration of death's feeding life expanded to include the care and feeding of the dead by the living. The practice of paying homage to past generations—the veneration of the ancestors—keeps that connection intact through the ages. We put our own paths into perspective by recognizing the trailblazers. To those who traveled this way before, we toast our thanks.

Here it is, the tobacco. I am certain that you, O ghost, are not very far away, that in fact you are standing right in back of me, waiting for me to reach you the pipe and tobacco, that you might take it along with you, that likewise you are waiting for your food to take on your journey.

"Prayer to the Ghost"
Winnebago

The Asian cult of the family is an extremely precious precept. The family group is primary in society. Each small grouping of relations is joined together with other such groups into larger and larger assemblies. The common threads that link them all is their one, mutual ancestor and the understanding that all of humankind is an extended family. In the season of gathering chill, Midsummer until Midfall, cultures throughout Asia celebrate some form of festival of death. In India, it is Pitra Visarjana Amavasya; in Laos, it is Ho Khao Padap Dinh; in Japan, it is Obon; and in Cambodia, it is Prachum Ben. In Vietnam, it is Trung Nguyen, Wandering Soul's Day; in pre-revolutionary

China, Chung Yüan, the Hungry Ghost Festival; in the People's Republic, Chieh Tsu, the Receiving Ancestors Festival.

"Oh, you who are our ancestors, who are departed, deign to come and eat!" the dead are called into supper in Cambodia on the Festival of the Dead. In Persia, food and drink were placed in the hall of the dead. The Dahomeys of West Africa prepare a harvest ritual called Setting the Table and invite the spirits of the ancestors. In Sicily as well, the table is set for those returning from the grave on I Morti, the Dead. Families in Mexico and parts of Italy hold picnics in the cemetery with the past generations right on their graves. A sort of breakfast in bed for the dead. Feasting the dead is evident in our language. The words "ghost" and "guest" both derive from the same Germanic root, *geist,* and were pronounced the same until only recently.

At festivals of the dead everywhere, special treats were featured for the enjoyment of those on both sides of the borderline of whatever it is that divides life and death, this world and the next. *Pan de muertos,* "bread of the dead," round sweet bread decorated on top with baked-dough bones and purple sugar, is baked once a year in Mexico on the Day of the Dead. In Germany, people consume *Seelenbrot,* "soul bread," to save a soul from purgatory. Italians eat sweets confected of egg white, chopped almonds, and sugar shaped like tibia and skeletons, *ossi da morto,* "bones of the dead." Sicilians bake elaborate ritual breads for the dead. *Armuzzi,* "souls of the dead," are shaped like two hands in repose, crossed over a breast, the fingers spread wide like wings.

At the halfway point of fall, when the nights were lengthening, when the winds from the north were subsiding and the Nile was sinking, the ancient Egyptians held the Isia. This six-day pageant commemorated the death of the corn god, the deity of crops and harvest in the personification of Osiris, son of Isis, the Earth Mother for whom the Isia is named. Participants masquerading as goddesses and gods reenacted the saga describing the death, disappearance, and rebirth of Osiris. Osiris dies in fall and is dismembered, as the grain is scythed and threshed. He is then resurrected as the corn in the spring. He is ultimately consumed as bread, coming to live again in the human lives that his loaves sustain. The story of the death of Osiris came to represent all the generations of the deceased. And the Isia was celebrated in honor of all departed souls.

On this night, the ancestors were invited back to their homes to join in an annual reunion of remembrance. Houses and paths were illuminated to lighten the dark way from the grave and back again and guide the ghosts safely to family and friends waiting in welcome. Altars were erected and tables laid with offerings of fine foods, flowers, and wine. The ghost-guests of honor were then feted with fabulous feasts of fealty.

> *Fall is the season of harvest and death.*
> *It also gets me hungry.*
>
> Armando Aranda
> Grade 5, P.S. 58

The traditions and ceremonial elements of this early Egyptian day of all souls, the Isia, traveled north and west through Greece and Rome to merge with those of the death cults of tribal Europe. When the Europeans pursued and amassed vast empires abroad, the festival of death went, too. The essential ceremonial symbols—the ghost, the mask, the fire, the food—have survived the centuries undiminished. They are the still-vital centerpieces of our own fall festival of death, Halloween.

Halloween descends from Samhain, the most significant holiday of the Celtic calendar, which revolves around eight major seasonal festivals corresponding to the solstices, equinoxes, and cross-quarter days. Being a pastoral people, the Celts counted their seasons according to the needs of their cattle and sheep, rather than the agricultural seasons farmers might mark. The year was divided into summer, when the herds are led out to graze, and winter, when they were brought back home again. Samhain, the day when the cows came home, was considered the first day of winter and also the first day of the New Year.

Samhain exposes a crease in time. A fissure between summer and winter. Between the old year and the new. During this period the dead have easy access to the living and are likely to pay a visit. As the herds returned home to the warmth and security of the hearth in winter, so, too, must the ghosts of the dead want to be cheered by familiar surroundings and loved ones.

> *All those who have lived in the past*
> *live in us now. Surely none of us would*
> *be an ungracious host.*
>
> Kahlil Gibran
> (Twentieth-century Lebanese)

Burial cairns were opened to release dead souls and air out the interiors of their tombs. The old ones were offered sacrificed animals, entertained, and fed in exchange for gifts of sweets from the underworld. In addition to the benign and beloved ghosts wandering about on Samhain, there were also innumerable fairies and goblins, strange specters and evil spirits released into the dark by Lord Samhain, Lord of Death.

For hundreds of years Christian missionaries tried without success to suppress Samhain and convert the Celts. In the eleventh century, Odilo, abbot at Cluny, claimed this heathen death feast for the church. Hallow Tide, Holy Time, is a three-day feast—All Hallows' Eve, All Hallows' Day, and All Saints' Day—during which prayers are offered for Christian saints and souls. Only Christian saints and souls. All others, those doomed souls whose burials were not consecrated in Christ, return to earth on the eve of All Hallows' to haunt the living. Menacing demons and flying witches with their trusty black cat sidekicks, the persistent practitioners of the pagan religion, were also out and about and up to no good.

Samhain was, above all, a fire festival. Indomitable, it blazed and burned undampened by the transparent overlay of Christianity. As in the Isia, fires were lit in aid of the dying sun. Torches and lanterns made from turnips guided the friendly ghosts where they wanted to go. And great bonfires were set to ward off any uninvited spooks and unsavory spirits.

> *From the ghoulies and ghosties and long-leggety beasties,*
> *And things that go bump in the night.*
> *Good Lord, deliver us!*

Cornish prayer

This tradition has been conscientiously upheld on a grand scale in Detroit, Michigan. Every year on Devil's Night, the night before Halloween, numbers of citizens faithfully set fire to abandoned buildings, trash piles, and junk heaps in an orgy of seasonal arson. The fires are most frequently set in vacant houses that pose a hazard to the community.

On Oidhche Shamhna, the Vigil of Samhain, in ancient Ireland, all fires were extinguished. A sacred new flame was sparked from which all other fires were rekindled and blessed. Until well into the nineteenth century, every village in the Scottish Highlands sported a fire called *samhnagen*, around which everyone danced. In Wales, every family lit a bonfire in front of their home. They placed a stone marked for each family member in the dying embers. In the morning, All Souls' morning, the stones were examined for omens for the coming year.

Other means of divination were also employed at Samhain, for it was felt that one might gain a glimpse of the future through the crack between the worlds with the helpful intercession of the ancestors and other sympathetic spirits. After a bobbed-for apple was caught in one's teeth, it was peeled in one long unbroken paring, then tossed without looking over the left shoulder. It would fall to the ground in the shape of the initial of one's true love. Apples and nuts were placed side by side in the fire representing two lovers. If they melted together and fused, it was a good sign for a happy marriage. If they popped and sparked and flew apart, it didn't auger very well for wedded bliss.

During Samhain, people outfitted themselves in masks and costumes as a sort of protection ritual, believing that one could successfully hide behind such a disguise and thereby escape bedevilment. In addition, as in the original masquerade of the Isia, their special apparel was intended to imitate and propitiate the deities. Fool them through flattery.

The potato famine of 1846 sent a million Irish immigrants to the United States. They brought with them their ancient Celtic customs, among them the feast of Samhain, which, as good Catholics, they now called Halloween. This shadow festival of soul survival struck a responsive chord in the American people, who instantly adopted it. To this day, Halloween is celebrated in some fashion by practically every person in North America. And the symbols—the ghosts, masks, fires, and food—are the same as they were thousands of years ago in Egypt.

The Spaniards, French, and Portuguese who landed in the Western Hemisphere brought with them a Latin version of All Souls' Day. Their customs merged with those of the Indians, who also observed a fall feast of the dead. On the Haitian midfall festival of death, the Guédé Mystères, the dead rise up from their graves, mount their spirit "horses," and enjoy life as incarnated souls. The Laguna Pueblo people visited the cemeteries to maintain the grave sites and to serve ritual feasts to the departed ones. It was also the practice of the Aztecs to attend to the graves of ancestors at Midfall. These were weeded and swept, markers scrubbed and painted. Most important of all, fresh flowers, sacred chrysanthemums, were presented in profusion to the dead. White for children and yellow for adults. It was also appropriate to offer chrysanthemums as the flower of the dead among the Creoles of New Orleans and throughout the Orient.

> *Deepen drop and die*
> *Many hued*
> *Chrysanthemums . . .*
> *One Black Earth for us all.*

> Ryusui
> (Japanese)

The amalgamation of the Aztec and Mexican traditions is Día de los Muertos. On the Day of the Dead, modern Mexicans, like their Aztec ancestors, gather to clean and decorate the cemeteries. They cleanse the atmosphere by lighting candles and copal on the gravestones. A picnic feast is then shared among the living and dead, recognizing no difference between them.

There is demonstrated on Día de los Muertos a most primal and personal identification with death. A palpable intimacy. People paint their faces as skeletons and go about their daily business. Special toys, dolls, and tableaus are sold depicting skeleton cops and skeleton banditos, skeleton bus drivers and skeleton baseball players, skeleton dentists and patients, brides and grooms, nuns and ballerinas, dogs and cats. Everybody has a skeleton.

This fact of life is sweetened with skeleton cookies and candies shaped like skulls, coffins, and gravestones. *Calaveras*, meaning "skulls" and "corpses," are greeting cards with teasing poems and cartoons, like funny valentines. These make fun of character flaws, foibles, and faulty political positions. All of which are ultimately, pitifully inconsequential, you see, because everyone is, after all, a *calavera* and dead already. Makes a person think.

Unfortunately, we Americans rarely—if ever—think about death if we can possibly help it. Perhaps we should. The greatest gift of the shadow of death is the challenge to really live life. With full consciousness. And conscience.

> *Death is coming,*
> *Life going*
> *The world is turning.*
> *People are starving.*
>
> K.L.N.
> Grade 3, P.S. 122

THE SUN

Come and I shall tell thee first of all the beginning of the sun and the sources from which have sprung all the things we now behold—the earth and the billowy sea, the damp vapor and the titan air that binds his circle fast round all things.

Empedocles
(Fifth-century-B.C. Greek)

The sun, sparkling jewel of the celestial crown, is actually a smallish, rather unspectacular star. Half the age of the Milky Way, it was born out of a cloud of gas a mere 5 billion years ago. It grew quickly into its familiar attributes and can be expected to enjoy a protracted middle age in a relatively unchanged state before the beginning of its eventual end. Though not a Hollywood star among stars, our sun is just that—ours. Of all the stars in all the galaxies, it is, at a distance of 93 million miles, our closest one. The one around which our world revolves. The light of our lives.

Insignificant within the perspective of all space as it may be, the sun, sovereign of our sky, seems spectacularly large to us. With a diameter of 864,000 miles, it is 109.5 times the diameter of earth. That relationship is the same as if the earth were scaled to pea-size and the sun were the size of a beach ball 130 feet across. Even though it's completely comprised of gas, it weighs 2 billion billion billion tons. Gravity on the surface of the sun is almost twenty-eight times greater than here on earth. This is like saying that if you could survive the intensity of a stroll on that astral oven, you would suddenly find yourself weighing two tons. The volume of the sun is 337,000 million million cubic miles, or 1.306 million times that of earth's.

The chemical composition of the sun and the earth is similar. However, there is no terrestrial comparison, our paltry attempts at nuclear combustion included, when it comes to producing power. The sun generates 400 trillion trillion watts of energy every second, enough energy to power 2,600 earths, each one entirely filled with 200-watt lightbulbs.

The temperature at its core, the focal inferno, is speculated to be 25 million degrees Fahrenheit. The sun's surface churns, roils, boils away, stirring up 6,000-degree heat bubbles, each the size of Pennsylvania. Its many-layered atmosphere surges to heights of 80,000 miles, and its corona reaches all the way to Mercury, 36 million miles away.

When it is hot I sweat alot.
When I sweat I feel the intense of heat.
Heat give off light.
Light give off energy.
Energy is give off of electricity.
Electricity give off shot.
Shot and then you get dead.

Denise Baque
Grade 6, P.S. 145

The sun, strongest, most potent of supernuminous powers, like any being, was born, lives, and shall one day die. In about 5 billion years it will start to expand, swell to become a red giant 166 times its present size. An inflatable hot-air atomic oven which will radiate dramatically increased heat. The ice caps on earth will melt, the oceans will evaporate, the deserts prevail. Venus will sizzle and Mercury will be cooked to a crisp.

Ultimately, that solar forge, that primary force, the source of all energy, will slip into gradual decline to what is called white dwarfdom, a cinder of its former fiery self. Fifty billion years from now, it will be a compressed black coal. Stone-cold dead. And, even after its demise, earth, though vastly changed and devoid of life as we know it, will continue its adoring circle dance round the sun.

In archaic times, people perceived the sun, in its shining prime and glory, the giver of heat and light and life, to be the effulgent force of the female. A passionate aspect of the Great Mother, the versatile jill-of-all-trades who issues forth and supports whole life. She is the Heaven-Illuminating Goddess, Amaterasu Omikami, in Japan, and the Queen of Heaven and Earth, Arinna, in Mesopotamia. She is Yhi, Sun Woman, to the Aruntas of Australia. Sun Sister was known in Anatolia, Siberia, and Native America.

Tribal northern Europe knew her, too. The Germans called her Sunna, as did the Norwegians. In Scandinavia, she was Glory-of-Elves or Sol. The *Eddas* say that on Doomsday she will bear a daughter who will be the new sun, the next creation, the luminous world to come. She was Sol, as well, to the Celts, who also called her Sul or Sulis. Her celebrations took place on open plains, on hilltops, overlooking springs. A major ceremonial site was Silbury Hill (Sulisbury Hill) adjacent to the springs at Bath, once called Aquae Sulis. The Romans dedicated the altars and sacred waters at Bath to Sul Minerva.

The Great Mother in ancient India was Aditi, the mother of the twelve spirits of the zodiac, the Adityas, who would "reveal their light at Doomsday." The *Mahanirvanatantra* describes the sun as a golden garment of light which graces the Great Goddess. "The sun, the most glorious symbol in the physical world, is the mayik vesture of Her who is 'clothed with the sun.'"

> Shamelessly
> orange like a
> parrot's beak,
> arousing with a lover's
> touch the clustered
> lotus buds
> I praise this
> great wheel the sun
> rising it is an
> earring for
> the Lady of the East.
>
> Vidya Kara
> (Eleventh-century Sanskrit)

Tantric Buddhist monks greeted the sun goddess, Marici, at dawn, chanting to her, "The glorious one, the sun of happiness ... I salute you, O Goddess Marici! Bless me and fulfill my desires. Protect me, O Goddess, from all the eight fears." Mari-ici, or Mari, was a precursor of the Christian Mary. The New Testament Book of Revelation refers to her as a "woman clothed in the sun."

Some early Christian mystics gazed upon the sun, the shining shawl that encircles Our Lady's shoulders, until they "became blinded by the light," for once having contemplated such magnificent brilliance, there was nothing left worthy of being seen. The success of this practice seems to have been a sure path to sainthood. An odd parallel is St. Lucy, Santa Lucia, Santa Luz, who plucked out her own eyes to discourage unwanted suitors and sexual advances. In the dark, with the One she truly loved, she was rewarded with the clear vision of the light of her faith.

The goddess was not always the sun herself, but often the force behind it. The grand controller of the cosmos, the sun, and the celestial cycles. According to Greek mythology, Leto laid an egg that produced two offspring, the sun and the moon, Apollo and Artemis.

With the advent of the patriarchy, the sun underwent a sex change. Profound, this gender shift was a portrayal of the left-brain revolution, the ascendance of reason over passion. Female divinity was overthrown, overthrone, overgrown, her domain plundered, her authority usurped, her worship polluted. The sun, with the strength of its brilliance, its sheer presence and potency, came to stand for the masculine principle, the power of rational thinking. The moon, reflective, more subtle, and seemingly erratic, came to be associated with the feminine in most cultures. Although the traits of the sun are thought to be male, it retains its female designation in the languages of northern Europe, Arabia, and Japan.

In Mesopotamian mythology, the Hittite sun goddess, Estan, evolved into Istanu, a male sun god. In pre-Islamic Arabia, the sun goddess was known as Torch of the Gods, Atthar or Al-llat. She was honored daily by pouring libations at rooftop altars. Her name was subsequently masculinized to Allah. Her other name, Shams, along with her attributes became associated with a male sun god, Shams-On. The Babylonian sun god was Shamash, clearly related. The Hebrew word for sun, as well as the appellation of the biblical character Samson, was also derived from her name.

The source of Samson's masculine strength was his long ray-like hair, which is symbolic of the sun. Other solar heroes, Apollo Chrysocomes (He of the Golden Locks) and Heracles, also wore streaming, gleaming tresses. Hathor, who birthed the sun, was depicted as the wild lion-maned sphinx.

Christ eventually became assimilated with other, older solar deities. There are many references that image him as the sun. Malachi, the Old Testament prophet, speaks as an oracle from God, "But for you who fear my name, the sun of righteousness shall rise with healing in his wings." This was taken by the early Christians to refer to the coming of Christ. Zachariah, father of St. John the Baptist, foretold Jesus' birth: "God . . . will send down to us the visit of the rising sun in order to illuminate those who are in the darkness and the shadow of death." Like Greek and Roman temples, the first churches were built with Eastern-oriented facades, and worshipers faced the East, the direction of the rising sun, while praying.

Because the sun is always there (in temperate and tropical climates, that is), it was deemed to be all-seeing, all-knowing, all-powerful. Omnipresence, omniscience, omnipotence. An eye is the symbolic expression of this concept. Several African tribes regard the sun as the eye of the supreme deity. The Samoyeds of the Arctic see the sun and moon as the eyes of heaven. Sulis, the name of the old Teutonic sun goddess, comes from *suil*, which means "the sun's eye." In Indian myth, the sun god, Sūrya, is the eye of Varuna, god of the heavens. In Greece, the sun, Helios, is the eye of Zeus; in Egypt, the eye of Ra; in northern Europe, the eye of Odin; in Oceania, the eye of Atea; and in Islam, the eye of Allah.

> *Thou eye of the Great God*
> *Thou eye of the God of Glory*
> *Thou eye of the King of creation*
> *Thou eye of the Light of the living*
> *Pouring on us at each time*
> *Pouring on us gently, generously*
> *Glory to thee thou glorious sun*
> *Glory to thee thou Face of the God of life.*

> "Song to the Sun," *Ortha nan Gaidheal*
> Traditional Gaelic

Since it determines both the cycle of the day and the circle of the seasonal year, the sun provides the structure of our existence, the framework within which our world revolves. As such, it seems to suggest all celestial and earthly regularity. Due to its dependability, the sun stands for law and order. Cosmic mandate. The sun Ra sailed through the skies accompanied by the goddess Maat, the embodiment of sunlight and the rightness of things, the natural order.

Civil law is an extrapolation of the structured order of the universe. Hammurabi, who in the eighteenth century B.C. codified Babylonian law, is always pictured standing on a stone column inscribed with the code of the king. He is facing Shamash, the sun, in whom justice dwells. It is Shamash who has sent down the law. Shamash was known as Great Judge of Heaven and Earth, and his Sun Temple was "the house of the judge of the world." Varuna was the guardian of the cosmic laws in Vedic India. He measured earth, sky, and air and cast the four directions. Sūrya, the sun, acted as his calipers.

While the sun is the seat of celestial order, organized government is the center of civic order. Sovereignty is established by the authority of the ruler of heaven. Royalty traditionally traces its lineage and aristocratic entitlement to the sun. Rule by divine right. The sun was the golden ancestor of the imperial families of ancient Egypt, India, Peru, and Mexico. The high chief of the Chumash people of old California was called *paha*, "image of the sun." The priest-chief who ruled the lower Mississippi Natchez theocracy was also the earthly representative of the sun, by whose sanction he commanded.

The emperor of Japan has always asserted descent from the sun goddess, Amaterasu Omikami. In 1946 the American occupation demanded that the emperor abolish the state religion and abdicate his own divine standing. He complied. Nonetheless, twice each year he continues to don the mantle of his inherited role of sun priest and prays for the well-being of his people in great ceremonies held at the Summer and Winter Solstices. The red sun still blazes in the center of the Japanese flag, proclaiming "The Land of the Rising Sun."

In Europe, too, kings and queens have claimed kinship to the cosmos. The first Christian emperor, Constantine I, was a sun worshiper. His coinage carried its radiant countenance along with a dedication to "the invincible sun, my guardian." In seventeenth-century France, Louis XIV, the Sun King, surrounded his court in solar imagery and gilded it in the pure gold of the sun as pronouncement of royal alliance with the Powers-That-Be. When Queen Elizabeth II of England was coronated in 1952, she wore a golden gown beneath her ceremonial robe. The officiating archbishop prayed that her throne "may stand fast in righteousness forevermore, like the sun before her and as the faithful witness in heaven."

Although the sun has been venerated to some degree in practically every culture in the world, a highly developed worship of the sun is comparatively rare. Solar cults flourished only in civilizations with vast civil structures and intricate political establishments that organized around a central source of absolute imperial authority. In these societies, social order revolved around the priest-king-chief in the same way that the earth revolves around the sun.

The Egyptians created the earliest and most elaborate of the sun cults. Sometime in the fourth millennium B.C., the moon calendar was discarded in favor of solar time telling. Gradually, the pantheon of local gods gained sunlike qualities and eventually coalesced into a supreme solar deity, Ra, whose worship was centered in Heliopolis (Sun City) in Lower Egypt. Through the pharaoh, his son, he ruled the world as he ruled the heavens. The order and rule of government, of society, indeed life itself, was deemed a direct inheritance from the sun. Divine dynasty. Solar symbolism is pervasive in Egyptian art, architecture, and literature.

To the entire world I give my light and my radiance; I give men warmth when they are cold; I cause their fields to fructify and their cattle to multiply; each day that passes I go around the world to secure a better knowledge of men's needs and to satisfy those needs. *Follow my example.*

> Inca myth
> Garcilaso de la Vega, *Royal Commentaries*
> (Sixteenth-century Spanish)

According to the records of the Spanish conquistadors, the Inca rule of Peru was one of the most organized and orderly regimes in the world. By the time of the European occupation, their empire reigned from Equador to northern Chile. All political, social, and religious organization was focused upon the Sun Temple in the center of Cuzco, the capital. The Incas considered themselves "children of the sun," whom they revered as Inti. The Palace of Gold, the shrine in honor of Inti, the sun from whom all riches flow, was lavishly decorated with that spectacular solar metal. It was situated so that each morning the rising sun would strike a gold-cast solar disk and bathe the entire interior with reflected yellow light.

The Aztec civilization of Mexico evolved into a solar monotheism as it became increasingly stable and affluent. Their ancestral tribal god, Huitzilopochtli, grew in influence and prominence and developed solar dimensions, as if to legitimatize their rule. The famous Aztec calendar, the "stone of the sun," diagrams the cosmology of the culture. In the center is the sun, Tonatiuh, He Who Goes Forth Shining. He is depicted as a bloodthirsty fellow, his great tongue stretched out to receive the ever-flowing "precious waters," the blood sacrifice, which he demands in payment for the great gifts he bestows upon the world. The literal lifeblood of the community must be regularly offered in exchange for energy. As it is the job of the sun to uphold the structure of the universe, it was the responsibility of the emperor to ensure that the world works well. To that end, Tonatiuh had to be properly propitiated.

Today we still offer ourselves up, well oiled, splayed on the altar of the sun. A rather snide sort of sacrament, actually, for such impudent adolescents to make. We have disdainfully rejected the gift of the sun's energy freely given and have, instead, overstepped the imperative of our species in our clumsy attempts to emulate holy conflagration. And we have burned our naughty little fingers in the process. But, perhaps, just perhaps, before we burn the house down around us, we will be able to learn, like any precocious child, not to play with fire.

> *Sun, my relative, be good coming out.*
> *Do something good for us.*
>
> *Make me work,*
> *So I can do anything I wish in the garden.*
> *I hoe, I plant corn, I irrigate.*

You, sun, be good going down at sunset.
We lie down to sleep. I want to feel good.
While I sleep, you come up.

Go on your course many times.
Make good things for us men.
Make me always the same as I am now.

"Prayer to the Sun"
Havasupai

THE MOON

☆—————————————————————————☾

The moon is a different thing to each of us.

Frank Borman, Apollo 8 astronaut
December 24, 1968

Like a bald baby or a two-year-old with dreadlocks dressed in
rompers, the moon has always attracted curiosity as to its gen-

der. Throughout time, people have created complex stories and scenarios about the sex of the moon. The man in the moon is a folkloric motif in much of the world. The Sanskrit name for moon, *mās*, is masculine, as is *māni*, the Norse. The moon is male in all Teutonic languages, and although the moon is sometimes referred to as female in English, French, Spanish, Italian, Latin, and Greek, the image that is commonly conjured is of the guy who hangs out up there.

Jewish Talmudic tradition holds that Jacob is in the moon, while French superstition tells that it is Judas Iscariot. He is Moon Man in Australia, Malaysia, and other parts of the South Pacific. Yue Lao is the Chinese Old Man in the Moon. He is the celestial matchmaker who predestines earthly marriages and binds together couples-to-be with lengths of red silk cord. The Serbian moon is called Myesyts in his guise as the Bald Uncle, but s/he is also referred to in the feminine familiar as the Pretty, Little One. The Chagas of Kenya see the paleness of lunar light as evidence that the Moon Chief and his followers are too backward to know how to use fire.

Roong is the male deity of the moon to the Haidas of western Canada. In his loneliness, he abducts a man to join him in the night sky. When, every so often, the captured man attempts to escape, he spills his pail of water, which rains down on the earth.

> *Scooping up the moon*
> *in the wash-basin,*
> *and spilling it.*
>
> Ryoho
> (Eighteenth-century Japanese)

The Swedish *Edda* describes the visible spots on the moon as a boy and a girl carrying a bucket of water. The children, Hjuki and Bil, have been adopted into our lexicon of legend as Jack and Jill. Their trudge up and consequent trip down the hill traces the monthly ascent and descent of the phases of the moon.

> *Jack and Jill*
> *went up the hill*
> *to fetch a pail of water.*
> *Jack fell down and*
> *broke his crown and*
> *Jill came tumbling after.*

Mother Goose

Many peoples blame the periodic changes in the vestige of the moon on his bad behavior. In Germany, the man in the moon carries a bundle of firewood or cabbages or sheep or straw, which he has stolen. In Europe of old, people thought that the dirty old man in the moon, with his parts fully engorged, impregnated women, making it unsafe to sleep in the moonlight. In a complete switch, Siberian Chukchi men exhibit their privates to the moon when they pray for her power.

Uaupe Indians of the Upper Amazon believe that a young woman's first menstruation is the result of her being deflowered by the moon. According to the Khasi tribes of the Himalayan Mountains, he keeps falling in inappropriate love with the mother of his wife, the sun. His monthly darkening is attributed to the ashes that his indignant mother-in-law hurls in his face in response to his offensive indiscretions.

> *The moon rises*
> *Stealing the Sun's light*
> *Between her thighs*

The man steals the nectar
between her thighs.

Folk song
Chhattisgarh, India

A similar tale is told among the Eskimos who inhabit the northernmost reaches of North America, Greenland, and Siberia. Here, the sun and moon, Malina and Anninga, are sister and brother. One night, Anninga secretes himself in his sister's chamber and surprises her in an impure embrace. Shocked but undaunted, she rubs soot on his face in the dark so that she might recognize her attacker by the light of day. The moon is thus found out. Rebuked, he must forever remain in the shadow of his sister's superior light.

Versions of this story are told throughout the Americas as far south as Brazil. In Romania, the roles are reversed. In this case, the moon is female. She dirties her own face with ashes to make herself unappealing in an attempt to repel the unwanted incestuous advances of her brother, the sun. According to Slavonic legend, the moon, the King of the Night, was unfaithful to the sun, who punishes him periodically for his transgressions. The Moon Man of the African Bushmen, too, incurs the wrath of the sun, who slices away at him, sliver by sliver, with a sword until he is completely destroyed. Exhausted after his ordeal, he has to go away to rest and regain his strength so that he may reappear the following month.

The early Egyptian moon god, Thoth, was depicted as an ibis or a dog-faced ape who was slowly eaten away by monsters as he made nightly voyages on his celestial barque. The Creek Indians believe the moon to be inhabited by an old man and his canine companion. The Salish of the Pacific Northwest see a toad in the moon, as do the Chinese, and the Angolan Moon King is associated with a frog. The Hindu moon god was known interchangeably as Soma, Indus, and Chandras. Consort of the stars, each of his twenty-seven stellar wives represented a lunar station. Chandras is most often shown carrying a hare.

The association of the rabbit with the moon traveled from India to China and Japan with the eastward spread of Buddhism. In China, it is thought that there is a hare on the moon who sits at the foot of a cassia tree grinding the powder of immortality in his mortar. When Ch'ang-O, the moon goddess, drank of this potion, she ascended to the moon and was transformed into a toad. In art, the moon is depicted as a white crescent along with a toad and a hare. The Japanese visualize a rabbit pounding rice with a pestle. The ideograms for the moon and for the milling of rice into flour for cakes are the same.

The Hottentots of southern Africa have a myth in which the moon beats a mischievous rabbit with a stick, giving it a harelip. The native people of old California called the moon the Great Rabbit. Julius Caesar relates that the ancient Britons considered the eating of rabbit taboo due to its lunar relationship. And, as recently as the 1970s, in Swabian Germany, children were forbidden from making hand shadows on the wall in the image of a bunny for fear of offending the moon. Rabbit's feet are still carried in sympathetic, if unconscious, moon-magic memory.

Most pre-Columbian Mexican codices picture the moon as a crescent-shaped water vessel in which the outlined profile of a rabbit can be seen. The lunar hare still prevails in the popular Mexican imagination. I remember looking out a window in a Mexico City suburb a few years ago straining the confines of my concentration in a futile attempt to make out the rabbit in the moon that my friends Alfredo and Alberto kept insisting was there. No matter how patiently, how persistently, they pointed it out, my unaccustomed eye simply could not perceive it.

I must confess that I never could recognize the face of a man in the moon, either. How could anyone conceivably mistake that face—that round, profoundly gentle face, jolly and eternally indulgent; that unconditionally comforting countenance—for male? The dark marks that define her features are the Sea of Tranquillity, the Ocean of Storms, and the Sea of Fertility. Sounds like a woman to me.

The hare is connected to the moon by virtue of her fertility cycle. Fecund, she fucks like a bunny, then thirty days later—roughly the time frame of one moon cycle—bears many babies. The hare is, in fact, related to the moon in the same way as is the female of every species. Her blood waxes and wanes with the moon, her urges and juices ebb and flow. And the moon, as it grows from crescent to full every month, mimics the pregnant swell of a bunny's belly, or a woman's, or a dog's.

> *Moon, O Mother Moon, O Mother Moon,*
> *Mother of living things,*
> *Hear our voice, O Mother Moon!*
> *O Mother Moon, O Mother Moon,*
> *Keep away the spirits of the dead,*
> *Hear our voice, O Mother Moon,*
> *O Mother Moon! O Mother Moon!*

Gabon Pygmy song

The moon as mother is a prevalent mythological theme, more primal than, and in many cases predating, that of the marauding male moon. The West African Nigers believe that the Great Moon Mother sends the Moon Bird to earth to deliver babies. The Bagandas of Central Africa bathe their newborns by the light of the first full moon following birth. In Ashanti tradition, the moon, Akua'ba, is a fertility figure. Women carry effigies of her tucked into their skirts at the small of their backs as an aid to conception and a guarantee of sturdy children.

Women in Europe did the same. During the Renaissance,

long after the mass acceptance of Christianity, it was understood that if a woman wanted anything, she should pray not to God, but to the Moon Mother for succor. St. Augustine denounced women for dancing "impudently and filthily all the day long upon the days of the new moon," even as their Hebrew sisters were scorned for wearing lunar amulets by the biblical prophets in Isaiah 3:18.

In Italy, even now, women engaged in the act of giving birth clutch crescent-shaped charms and pray to Mary, Mother of God, for help. The Virgin Mary is frequently displayed standing upon a crescent moon. The Greek Hera, Demeter, Artemis, Thetis, Phoebe, and Selene; the Roman Luna, Mana, and Diana; Gala or Galata of the Gaelic and Gaulish tribes—all were associated with the moon, and as her handmaidens, they aided women in labor.

> . . . *I standing on your crescent, madonna, moon,*
> *Old woman that never dies, being perpetually*
> *Renewed, made nothing again, made small again,*
> *Waxing again, going through it all over again,*
> *I would lift up my song, bark, howl, bay to you;*
> *I would say to you, remember me, beloved 3-headed nurse,*
> *I have swallowed your milk, you wiped me and wrapped me;*
> *Beautiful motherly monster, watch over me still.*

> Constance Urdang
> (Twentieth-century American)

The Egyptian hieroglyph transcribed as *mena* means both "moon" and "breast." Hathor, the sky goddess, is the Celestial Cow and is depicted as carrying the moon disk between her horns. From her breasts flow the stars and Milky Way. Britain was originally called Albion after the milk-white moon goddess, until, that is, the monk Gildas succeeded in transforming her into a fictitious male St. Alban. The European continent is named after the goddess Europa, who was also known as Hera and Io, the White Moon Cow.

The first woman of Polynesia was the moon, Hina, and each woman thereafter is a *wahine*, created in her image. The Finnish creatrix was known as Luonnotar, Luna the Moon. It was she who gave forth the great World Egg from which hatched the entire universe. The Peruvian moon was Mama Quilla. She, too, bore an egg. Mama Ogllo, the Moon Maiden, along with her brother, the sun, founded the royal Inca dynasty. The Zunis of the American Southwest venerate the Moon Our Mother, who is the younger sister of the sun. To the Apaches and the Nava-hos, she is Changing Woman. The Sioux call her the Old Woman Who Never Dies. To the Iroquois, she is the Mother Who Created the Earth and the Surface People.

The moon, as Queen of Heaven, reigned in the Near East: Babylonia, Persia, Syria, Sumeria, Arkadia, and Canaan. She From Whom All Life Issues was known as Anath, Asherath, An-ahita, Qadesh, Lilith, Ishtar, Inanna, and Astarte, which means "womb." As Ishtar, she sings, "I the mother have begotten my people and like the young of the fishes they fill the seas." In pre-Islamic Arabia, the moon was feminine and her cult prevailed. She was Manat, the Moon Mother of Mecca, and her shrines are still holy, although women are constrained from entering them. Another of her names, Al-lat, was altered at the advent of the pa-triarchy to become Allah. By Muhammad's order, all religious amulets must be made with silver, her special metal.

> *The glow and beauty of the stars*
> *are nothing near the splendid moon*
> *when in her roundness she burns silver*
> *about the world.*
>
> Sappho of Lesbos
> (Seventh-century-B.C. Greek)

The moon continues to reign supreme, her sovereign image ever-widely proudly proclaimed. The crescent moon, alone or with one or more stars, is today displayed on the flags of Turkey, Pakistan, Tunisia, Libya, Algeria, Malaysia, Singapore, Northern Cyprus, Nepal, the Maldives, and South Carolina. The moon displayed on the flag of Palau in the South Pacific is full and golden, glorious against a field of sea-blue sky.

The moon herself was impaled by an American flag over a quarter of a century ago. That proud standard, those bright stars and bold stripes (artificially splinted) fly forever erect, waving aloft in a windless world. Lifeless, they lend mute testimony to the all-time-hands-down most outrageous stud challenge ever. And so the Man in the Moon, the Mother in the Moon, the Maid in the Moon, and all the sundry lunar pets have now, in this era of mass-media consciousness, been replaced, far surpassed, by that vastly impressive, permanently indelible collective image of the Man Walking on the Moon.

> *Who (said the moon)*
> *Do you think I am and precisely who*
> *Pipsqueak, who are you*
>
> *With your uncivil liberties*
> *To do as you damn please?*
> *Boo!*
>
> *I am the serene*
> *Moon (said the moon).*
> *Don't touch me again.*
>
> *To your poking telescopes,*
> *Your peeking eyes*
> *I have long been wise.*
> *Science? another word*
> *For monkeyshine.*
> *You heard me.*

Get down, little man, go home,
Back where you come from,
Bah!

Or my gold will be turning green
On me (said the moon)
If you know what I mean.

   Robert Francis
   (Twentieth-century American)

THE STARS

I have . . . a terrible need. . . . shall I say the word? . . . of religion. Then I go out at night and paint the stars.

Vincent van Gogh
(Nineteenth-century Dutch)

When I was in the fourth grade, the teacher assigned us the
writing of a poem for homework. Normally, I was a quite dil-

igent student, but that evening it didn't occur to me to sit down with paper and pencil and purposefully spin a poem. Instead, impelled by a mysteriously improbable impulse eons beyond my normal range of rationality, I *knew* that if I were to go outside in the middle of the night alone, I would *get* my poem.

Outside? At night? Alone? Absurd. The very idea was completely inconceivable to this usually obedient child. Yet, despite the odds, I was propelled forward by an incontrovertible passion, compelled by some primal instinct of survival, to follow my own inner promptings. So, in my first inspired act of conscious rebellion in pursuit of my spiritual self, I secretly stayed awake until everyone was asleep, then sneaked triumphantly outside to stand by myself beneath a billion stars. Aglow with the radiant magic of the moment, I was rewarded for my resolution with tranceformation.

The poem, of course, did come—of its own accord and completely composed. "As I lie beneath the sky, I look above and wonder why . . ." Exhilarated and starry-eyed, empowered by the authority of this celestially auspicious experience, I remained awake the rest of the night reciting it again and again to memorize it rather than risk discovery by turning on the light to write it down. Interestingly, this is the very process of enchantment employed by the Siberian shamans I would read about decades later, who *hear*, rather than compose, their power songs, then claim them through repeated use. "As I lie beneath the sky, I look above and wonder why . . ."

Another version of my own innocent query by nineteenth-century British writer Jane Taylor became famous:

> *Twinkle, twinkle, little star*
> *How I wonder what you are.*
> *Up above the world so high*
> *Like a diamond in the sky.*

Twinkle, twinkle, little star.
How I wonder what you are.

What indeed? From the point of view of modern astronomy and physics, stars are spheres of hot gas born of the condensation from giant, diffuse, vaporous cloud complexes. These gaseous round bubbles are self-inflated and are kept from collapsing by their own internally generated thermal force. They are pumped up and pressure-cooked by the continuous hydrogen-bomb-like nuclear reactions in their infernal cores. When their lifetime supply of fuel is exhausted, they die.

Since the intensity of their heat diminishes with age, the color of a star can indicate its stage of life. Blue orbs are brilliant; young and intensely hot. Some supernovae are as bright as the entire galaxy that houses them. Yellow stars like our sun have cooled a bit by their middle age. Mellow yellow. Red stars are dim; feeble and elderly. Black holes and white dwarfs, stars that are near their inevitable death, are so dark as to be invisible from as close as a few miles away.

Each star dances to its own individual drummer. Some display a steady light, calm and sedate, a stately countenance; others flicker and twitter about like birds in barely contained agitation; and still others signal in unending, unchanging, blinking-blinking rhythm. Some rotate in a seemly manner and some do a dervish spin. Some stars perform solo, our own sun, *el sol*, for one. But most share the stage with one or more partners. Duo tangos are quite common. In this case, the two stars orbit each other, sometimes coming so close that "star stuff," as Carl Sagan calls it, is exchanged. Stellar dirty dancing.

The blanket of stars seemed thick to me as a child standing in a dark suburban backyard; their numbers untold. While there are thought to be well over 300 billion stars in the galaxy.

The vast majority are so far away they are beyond our visual range. Some are obscured by interstellar dust. Only about 2,000 stars are visible to the naked eye. With an amateur telescope it is possible to see perhaps 1 million stars. Even through the sights of the most sophisticated telescope we are privy to a mere 100 million. And our galaxy, as astronomically enormous as it is, is but one associate member of the universal society of galaxies, 100 billion strong. There are as many galaxies in the universe as there are stars in the sky! At *least*.

Stargazing was one of humankind's first fascinations. Imagine the awesome specter of the sky in the vast pitch of the pre-smog night before electricity, before even fire. The heavens were alive with shimmering spots of light streaming slowly and ever so silently across the clear celestial ceiling. The choreographed multitude of stars in such apparent proximity provided a never-ending source of speculation, investigation, and inspiration. Only in a remote desert or high on an isolated mountain can we moderns experience such a staggering view.

We had the sky, up there, all speckled with stars, and we used to lay on our backs and look up at them, and discuss about whether they was made, or only just happened.

Mark Twain
(Nineteenth-century American)

The original people of south-central Australia attribute the presence of the "fires in the sky" to Star Woman, who threw coals from her fire into the stratosphere one dark, moonless night. According to Navajo tradition, the people stitched the stars onto the heavens which the old wise ones had created. They took great pride in designing beautiful and complex patterns. Then Wolf came along and mocked their precision: "Why so much fuss over a bit of embroidery? Why not just stick the stars anywhere about the sky?" And he proceeded to scatter them randomly.

To the Egyptians, the stars were spirit homes, gathering sites for the souls of the blessed. The Turko-Tatar tribes, who live in yurts, describe the sky as a huge and majestic tent. The Milky Way is the seam at the top that holds it together, and the stars are holes in its sides. Other peoples have associated the mysterious stars as viewing holes, like pinpoint projectors, which allow us to glimpse at the source of the celestial flame. "They came to a round hole in the sky . . . glowing like fire. This, the Raven said, was a star," relates an Eskimo creation myth.

> O burning light of the stars,
> O most splendid model of the regal nuptials,
> O glowing jewel!
> You are arrayed as a high ranking woman
> with neither stain nor fault.

> Hildegard von Bingen
> (Twelfth-century German)

The Yakut people of the Siberian steppe see the stars as crystal windows through which we are watched by the gods. "Let the windows of heaven be opened," commanded Yahweh in the Old Testament story of the Flood. Native New Zealanders believe that the stars are the eyes of wandering spirits. Indra, the Hindu Lord of the Firmament, is depicted as wearing a cloak covered with eyes. The old Mexican symbol of the heavens is a semicircle sprayed with eyelike imagery.

In Norse myth, the steady morning star turns out to be the frozen toe of a certain hero, Orwandill, which had been tossed into the sky by the thunder god, Thor. The Omahas of the North American Great Plains say that the North Star is the Star That Does Not Walk Around, and the Arapahos call it the Fixed

Star. Certain Eskimos talk about the sky as the dark grass of night which is scattered with glittering star-lakes. The Sumerians called them the shining herd, as do the Lethape Phatsimo of Botswana, still. Venus was associated with the goddess Ishtar, who was known to the Semitic tribes as the Holy Heifer.

Venus, universally regarded as a particularly spectacular star, notable for preceding the rising sun each day or following the setting sun each night, bore a bevy of names bestowed upon her by admirers the world over. She was Ishtar in Chaldea, Isis in Egypt, Nanbu in Babylonia, Benu in Sumeria, Anahita in Persia, Astarte, then Aphrodite in Greece, Quetzalcóatl in Aztec Mexico, Kukulcán in Mayan Mexico, Hoku-loa in ancient Hawaii, and Ta'urua in Tahiti.

She was Queen of Heaven, Morning Star, Evening Star, Guiding Star, Wasp Star, Red Star, Great Star, Lone Star, Star of Prophesy, the Shining One, Mother of Deities, She Who Possesses the Law of Heavenly Sovereignty, Bringer of Light, Home of the Love Goddess, Proclaimer, Lord of the Dawn, Companion to the Royal Inebriate.

> *O Ishtar, Sovereign Mistress of all people,*
> *You are the light of heaven and earth;*
> *heaven and earth move because of you.*
> *All people pay homage to you*
> *for you are great, you are exalted.*
> *All humankind recognizes your power,*
> *for you are the bright torch of heaven and earth,*
> *the light of all living.*
> *One who cannot be possessed,*
> *whirlwind that roars against all that is wrong.*
>
> Mesopotamia, 5000 B.C.
> (Reworked by Merlin Stone in
> *Ancient Mirrors of Womanhood*)

The ancients had an intimate understanding of the patterns and pathways of the stars. They organized the legions of individual stars into recognizable geometric arrangements to facilitate easier identification. Onto these stellar shapes, they projected images of animals and objects with which they identified and which reflected their cultural interests, outlooks, and occupations. They installed god/desses-in-residence and peopled them with s/heroes of myth and legend.

Although different peoples perceived different permutations, a few particularly singular shapes are distinguished widely: the hunter, Orion, who sports a splendid belt of three shiny celestial stones; Taurus, the bull, which incorporates the popular Pleiades asterism (a distinctive star group within a star group); Gemini, which features the star twins, Castor and Pollux; and most famous of all, Ursa Major, in which the Big Dipper, another asterism, can be located.

The Milky Way is recognized everywhere on Earth. The Bushmen of the African Kalahari Desert see the Milky Way as the Backbone of the Sky. Swedes call it the Winter Street Which Leads to Heaven. To the Norse, it is the Path of Ghosts; to the Indians of Patagonia in Argentina, it is the White Pampas Where Ghosts Hunt Rheas (flightless birds of the grasslands). Australian Aborigines say that it is the Rising Smoke of a campfire in the sky. The Pawnees call it Path of the Dead or, much more prosaically, Stream with Scum Extending. To the Navajos, it is Which Awaits the Dawn, to the Cherokees, Where the Dog Ran, and to the Chumashes, Journey of the Piñon Gatherers.

> *We are the stars which sing*
> *we sing with our light.*
> *we are the birds of fire*
> *we fly over the sky,*
> *our light is a voice.*
> *we make a road for spirits,*
> *a road for the Great Spirit.*
> *amongst us are three hunters*

who chase a bear.
there never was a time
when they were not hunting;

we look down on the mountains,
this is the song of the stars.

"Song of the Stars"
Passamaquoddy

The boundaries of these star formations are arbitrary. The exact outlines of the Constellations differ from society to society, as do their descriptive appellations. In the days of the great hunters, the nighttime sky was teeming with bears, dogs, women, hunters and their implements. When in the seventeenth century European sailors first saw the constellations of the southern sky, they named them after the tools of science: compasses, telescopes, microscopes, and the sterns of sailing ships.

Today the International Astronomical Union ratifies star names, both old and new. Since they are used by scientists around the globe, official star designations are often simply catalog numbers, devoid of cultural context, although romantics with stars in their eyes and a mere forty dollars in their pockets can (allegedly) arrange to have a star named for them. Advertising this service as an ideal gift for any occasion, one private company has sold hundreds of thousands of misleading certificates to purchasers, claiming to have registered a star in their name.

In the years since I was that star-struck kid, our planet has suffered a particularly noxious pollution in the insidious form of light poisoning. It simply never gets dark anymore. Just a quarter of a century after my stellar initiation, I would hurry home loaded with sky charts and maps, inspired by my classes at the Hayden Planetarium and eager to practice my ability to identify constellations and planets. Time and again I'd run up to the roof only to realize once more that the stars in New York City are not necessarily in the sky.

We in urban areas—which is most everyone on earth these days—are constantly surrounded by inescapable ambient light which obliterates our view of the heavens and deprives us of a personal relationship with the universe. Over the years, I have had occasion to accompany groups of the biggest, baddest inner-city youth to the country for various field outings. It was always the same story, amusing in a bittersweet sort of way. These brutes, these poor babes, inevitably would refuse to get off of the bus because they were *afraid of the dark*. Never in their entire lives had they been in the dark. Or seen the stars in the sky.

This is beyond sad, this is tragic. And the consequences are potentially disastrous. *Disastrium* in Greek; *disastrato* in Latin. *Dis* means "torn away from or apart from," and *astrato* means "the stars." Our kids know that. They are perfectly right to be pissed at being dissed.

> Among all the strange things that men have forgotten, the most universal and catastrophic lapse of memory is that by which they have forgotten that they are living on a star.
>
> G. K. Chesterton
> (Twentieth-century English)

TOTAL ECLIPSE OF THE SUN

Eclipses have always, everywhere, caused intense emotional un-easiness for people who are aware that the heavenly bodies are not as they should be. That all is not right with the world. The world, in fact, is upside down, with everything appearing to be its own upsetting opposite. A solar eclipse is only possible when the moon is new—the very time when it is normally invisible. But because the moon is silhouetted against the sun as it slides by, we are able to see it. And we can see it in the daytime. The passage of the moon in front of the sun transforms that sphere into a crescent shape which mimics that of the moon. Light and heat diminish as we are separated from the direct rays of the sun, making day seem like night. Reality is reversed. Could this not signal the end of the world?

> *Nothing in the world can surprise me now.*
> *Nothing is impossible or too wonderful.*
> *For Zeus, father of the Olympians,*
> *has turned midday into black night*
> *by shielding light from the blossoming sun,*
> *and now dark terror hangs over mankind.*
> *Anything may happen, so do not be amazed if beasts*
> *on dry land seek pasture with dolphins in*
> *the ocean, and those beasts who loved sunny hills*
> *love crashing seawaves more than the warm main land.*

> Archilochus, "An Eclipse of the Sun,"
> (Seventh-century-B.C. Greek)

Consider the specter of an unexpected, unexplained eclipse of the sun. How completely terrifying it must be if, without warning, it just happened one day. The light gradually weakens as the moon crosses the sun disk, but, strangely, the sky remains clear blue. Just before totality, the shadow of the moon bears down at a terrifying speed of two thousand miles per hour. A whoosh of a wind and then the air becomes unusually still. Birds and animals, even insects, hush. Certainly, most definitely, this *must* mean the end of the world! But, then, within minutes, a new dawn breaks. The birds start the day all over again, their songs a sigh of relief.

"Eclipse" comes from the Greek *ekleipsis*, meaning "to fall out of place, to fail, to forsake, to abandon." Yes, the sun abandons us to the dark, but why? The most common cross-cultural mythological interpretations of eclipses have been in terms of embattlement: the defeat, devouring, or death of one of the heavenly bodies usually ascribed to some evil supernatural agency. There was actually a period in ancient Rome when it was held to be blasphemous and even illegal to speak openly of an eclipse being a natural phenomenon. What, after all, is *natural* about an eclipse?

The most widespread explanations had heavenly monsters and beasts pursue the sun and try to kill it. In China and Thailand, the monster is the Heavenly Dragon. In old Germanic tribes and among some North American Indians, the culprits are dogs, wolves, and coyotes. In Norse myth, it is a supernatural wolf. In South America, the beast is the jaguar. In Africa and Indonesia, they are snakes. And in India, they are the star demons, Rahu and Ketu. Amaterasu, the Japanese sun goddess, was forced to retreat into the depths of a cave to escape the violent outbursts of her brother, Susu-wo-no, the imperious storm god. In Babylonian myth, the ecliptic period of darkness was caused by the invasion of the vault of heaven by seven devils. The Tatars said the sun was attacked by a vampire who lives in the stars. The African Dahomeys talk of the sun and the moon being locked in war.

Although panic-stricken in the face of an eclipse, these people rallied together in protection of the sun. They set out to create an incredible clamorous uproar loud enough to scare away the savage sky beasts. They beat their drums and pots and kettles. They banged rocks together and cymbals. They rang bells. They yelled. They shouted and wailed. They set off fireworks. They sent fire arrows screaming into the sky. Some even danced to save the life of the sun by circling around a smoldering fire of old clothes and hair. The stench rises and causes the devouring creature to sneeze and so disgorge the sun.

Come out, throw sticks at your houses
come out, turn your buckets over . . .
look all around the world, dance, throw your sticks,
help out, look at the moon.

Alsea moon eclipse exorcism

Other North American tribes, the Hottentots of Africa, the Ainus in Japan, and the Minangkabaus in Sumatra see the sun as suffering from a fainting sickness. The Ojibwas imagined that the sun was being extinguished and so sent flaming torches into the sky to rekindle the one dropped. The Chilcotin Indians tucked up their robes, and then, leaning on sticks, they walked in circles until the eclipse was over, sympathetically encouraging the exhausted sun to continue its sky journey. Similarly, in Egypt, the pharaoh, representative of the sun, walked solemnly around the walls of the temple to ensure that the sun would perform its daily journey uninterrupted by an eclipse.

Some more benign eclipse explanations come from the Eskimos, Aleuts, and Tlingits of Arctic America who believe that the sun has left its celestial position in order to check on how things are going on earth. Still other American Indian peoples envision the sun as cradling her/his child in an embrace. In Tahiti, the sun and moon are seen to be making love, obscuring each other as they tumble about in the sky. In these instances, understanding and indulgent but prudent people buried embers for the duration of the eclipse to ensure that all fire would not be lost.

Tribal peoples who live in direct communion and cooperation with the natural world feel a physical kinship and identification with the celestial bodies. A disruption of the normal course of nature such as an eclipse boded the worst sort of personal danger for people. The Aztecs thought that if a child was born at the time of the eclipse biting the sun, it could similarly bite the child with a harelip or permanently shadow its face with a birthmark. The Mayan *Dresden Codex* lists potential eclipse days as "Woe to the maize!" and "Woe to pregnant women!"

> *The fire darkens, the wood turns black.*
> *The flame extinguishes, misfortune upon us.*
> *God sets out in search of the sun.*
>
> Hottentot

The Babylonians discovered that there is a cycle, or *saros*, of 233 intervals between new moons after which eclipses of the same family recur. Every eighteen years, ten days, and seven-plus hours, eclipses of the same family type repeat themselves but at a different location and can therefore be predicted. The ability to tell when an eclipse would occur meant that it was possible to prepare ritual measures to ensure safe passing of the eclipse and a speedy return of the sun.

For the Chinese, an eclipse signaled a grave omen of governmental misrule and disaster which must be averted at all costs. According to legend, two official court astronomers, Hsi and Ho, were once taken by surprise by an eclipse they had failed to predict, no doubt because they had gotten themselves drunk. This resulted in their being unprepared to perform the proper protective rites, the efficacy of which was uncontested. So, even though the eclipse passed and the sun recovered from its attack by the Celestial Dragon, the two astronomers were put to death anyway, their heads chopped off as a lesson by Chung K'ang, fourth emperor of the Hsia dynasty. Indeed, the Chinese have never failed to accurately predict an eclipse since.

The earliest recorded eclipse was that of October 22, 2136, B.C., as stated in the ancient Chinese classic *Chou King*, or *Book of History*. An early well-documented use of the *saros* cycle was by Thales of Miletus, the Greek scientist and statesman. According to Herodotus, Thales predicted the solar eclipse of May 28, 585, B.C., which occurred during a battle between the Medes and the Lydians. Its opportune occasion caused the cessation of hostilities and was followed by a continued peace.

Christopher Columbus was able to profit from his foreknowledge of the lunar eclipse of April 2, 1493, when he threatened the indigenous inhabitants of Jamaica with divine vengeance when they refused to supply his ships. He told them that that very night the moon would fail to light the sky. His son Ferdinand describes the event in his journal:

> At the rising of the moon the eclipse began, and the higher the moon rose the more the eclipse increased. The Indians observed it, and were so frightened that with cries and lamentations they ran from every side to the ships, carrying provisions, and begged the Admiral by all means to intercede for them with God that he might not make them feel the effects of his wrath, and promised for the future, diligently to bring all he had need of.

A letter to the *Philadelphia Inquirer* describes the solar eclipse of July 29, 1878, as

> the grandest sight I ever beheld but it frightened the Indians badly. Some of them threw themselves upon their knees and invoked the Divine blessing; others flung themselves flat on the ground, face downwards; others cried and yelled in frantic excitement and terror. Finally one old fellow stepped from the door of his lodge, pistol in hand, and fixing his eyes on the darkening sun, mumbled a few unintelligible words and raising his arm took direct aim at the luminary, fired off his pistol, and after throwing his arms about his head in a series of extraordinary gesticulations, retreated to his own quarters.

As it happened, that very instant was the conclusion of totality.

Today it isn't a question of us trying to frighten away the eclipse. Or to be frightened by it, either. The critical thing for us of the urban persuasion is to take the time to notice it at all. The danger we face is not from the sky, but from our own distraught disconnectedness. The sun has not abandoned us. We have abandoned the sun, turning it into our own ozoneless enemy. We have abandoned our own mother, the earth. And the moon as well, which still sports an American flag, a golf ball, and a footprint left behind by the good ole boys on their walk. Think of that for a moment when the moon eclipses the sun. What a metaphor.

Even when an eclipse is a partial one from our geographic point of view, it offers us a rare glimpse of these majestic phenomena. Partial means "incomplete." A slim glimpse of an awesome sky show in its entirety. But partial also means "taking sides, taking a part." Let us truly take part in the next eclipse. Take the time to note its passing. Let the notion of darkening skies remind us of our critical response-ability to the planet. And then, when the sun is restored again, let us celebrate a new dawning of our own dedication and, yes, partiality. As in "having a special affection for." Let us be partial to the sun. To the sky. To the whole living earth. And each other.

On July 11, 1991, there was a total eclipse of the sun. The following is from my eclipse journal, El Gran Eclipse de México, July 11, 1991:

After writing about its coming, my own particular partiality persuaded me that I should travel to Mexico to see it for myself. Total solar eclipses are likely to occur in any location on the globe only once in every 360 years. Stay-at-home gazers have to be really lucky. It's true that the next total eclipse to be seen in North America will actually be centered in Cleveland, Ohio, my hometown. In 2017, I'll be seventy-two and can return, the prodigal daughter, to celebrate the forty-second anniversary of Celestially Auspicious Occasions. But I can't count on it.

I didn't buzz down to Baja, hyped by the media to be the best viewing place because of the abundance of resort rooms nearby. I went instead with my old pilgrimage partner, Sarah, to what would be the epicenter of longest totality, according to the Planetarium. We trekked to Tepic, Nayarit, near the western coast of Mexico. But where to watch from? Certainly not from the plaza of this rather unlovely city where we had been some years before. We scoured the map for a likely place, secluded and wild, a special setting for this exceptional event.

We found it. La Laguna de Santa María del Oro. The name alone was appropriate. After all, the pre-Columbian civilizations of Central and South America associated the radiant sun with *oro*, gold. And Santa María stands for the female forces of the universe, the goddess who was, is, and ever will be. *La laguna* itself, high in the mountains, is a three-kilometer-round lake that fills the crater of an extinct volcano. The Lacandón Indians, direct descendants of the Mayans, used to watch eclipse shows in a pan of water. We would have a lake. What more could we want?

No sooner did we buy our nonrefundable tickets than I remembered that July was the height of the rainy season. Would clouds and rain obscure the eclipse? Would we really be able to see anything? Was this total folly? We went and we prayed. Immediately upon takeoff in Dallas, we were surrounded by huge thick dense masses of clouds. I didn't think anything of it at the time, it was simply a beautiful sky sight. But when we landed in Puerto Vallarta, the clouds did, too.

Puerto Vallarta was plastered with posters about El Gran Eclipse '91—viewing tips, safety warnings, scientific information. There was an energy buzz of excitement and expectation everywhere in town. There was also so much cloud cover that we couldn't see the stars. Next morning we bussed north to Tepic. There, too, signs were all over warning people not to look directly at the sun. We bought some special viewing glasses approved by the government to be safe. I desperately wanted to see this eclipse, but I didn't want it to be the last thing I ever saw.

Tepic, too, was very cloudy and it rained all day as it had in P.V. With every hour it seemed less likely that we would be able to see anything at all. That night the sunset was brilliant red and I couldn't remember if that meant the next day would be clear or stormy. I knew what I wanted, so I took it to mean blue skies to come, even though it seemed pretty improbable given the weather to date. But after coming so far, I certainly had to hope.

The next day we caught a 6 A.M. pig and chicken bus up the mountain to *la laguna*, and as we were leaving town it actually appeared as if it might clear. But as we started the slow ascent, we drove deeper and deeper into the gray, leaving the un-clouded skies behind. Every kilometer closer that we came to our goal, the darker it got, until, once again, it began to rain. We joked and laughed, channeling our growing disappoint-ment. The Mexican family across the aisle were infinitely more philosophical. After all, either we would see it or we wouldn't. It was out of our hands.

We crossed the guardian peaks ringing the volcano and emerged from the thick clouds into a shining blue Shangri-La, both lake and sky. Could this be true? Would we be blessed? *¿Quién sabe?* Three and a half hours would tell. We couldn't help but allow ourselves to begin to believe in the best. Chances, all of a sudden, seemed good. This was our first glimpse of the sun since we had landed in Mexico four days ago.

We walked around the lake until we came to a beach area that had been cleared of trees, an opening in the dense ground cover. From here we would have an expansive view of sky and lake. The water had too much movement to reflect the eclipse well. Sarah dug a hole in the dirt, lined it with a plastic bag held in place with stones, and then filled it with water. This basin served as a smooth-surfaced mirror, which perfectly showed the sun. We also made a series of pinhole projectors of various sizes. We loaded our cameras. We had our official eye protector goggles. We were ready.

We could only estimate, because this tiny remote place wasn't listed on any of the timetables, but it was nearing time for first contact. I looked through one of the pinholes and there, plain as day, I could see that a tiny slice had been shaved from the right side of the sun. It had started and the sky was blue! We could see! Had we stayed in New York City, this is all we would have been able to see—if we were able to see it at all. The East Coast would experience only about a 2 percent partial eclipse. And here we were, just settling in for the whole show, the longest eclipse for the rest of the century.

When I looked directly at the sun through the Mylar glasses, I could see that a slice had been carved from the left side. I should have realized that both our wishing-well pot of water and the pinhole devices project a reverse image. The process of the eclipse was slow and mesmerizing. The sun disk disappeared by centimeters, it seemed. Reduced, halved, quartered, cut into the slimmest crescent, exactly like the moon each month. The skies were beginning to darken very slightly. Was it the eclipse or that bank of black storm clouds climbing to meet the shrinking sun? It was a sky contest now.

All of a sudden, when the sun was a slight crescent and it was still quite light, a wild wind rose up, blowing the trees and churning the waters. Now, I knew very well about this wind which always happens before the period of totality. I knew to expect it. But the birds were shrieking in hysterical panic, and that sent a chill up my spine. And then, in a split second, the sun was gone. It was instantly dark. I guess I thought it would be gradual. It was pitch-black and chill and utter stillness. Then the night sounds descended in an instant. Cicadas and frogs were chattering away, wondering, no doubt, what happened to their daytime sleep.

Was the sun behind a cloud? We couldn't see to tell. But no, there it was! I could see it clearly now: the sun's fiery corona surrounding the black circle cast by the backlit moon. This is really it. We screamed, we danced, leaped around, laughed, cried. We grew silent. The majesty was beyond expression. The experience, all.

I stripped off my dress and ran into the water. And there I was, naked, floating on my back in the warm waters of this lake in the sky, in this volcano, on this mountain, on this glorious earth, watching this utter miracle. I felt myself to be very small, but secure in the energetic embrace of our wondrous universe. And then, as if there could possibly be more than this, there was indeed more. We were able to see several bright red plumes shoot off the surface of the sun and dance around the perimeter, followed by the diamond necklace effect every astronomer hopes for.

It was almost too much to take in. And, indeed, as if it really was too much, at the exact instant of the conclusion of totality the clouds broke and the rains descended. The show was over. We trudged back around to the *palapa* restaurant/bus stop. As we waited for the evening bus down the mountain, we watched the progress of the eclipse on TV on the patio as it made its way south through the rest of Mexico, Central and South America. We ate fish from the lake and drank beers. Sated, as from the world's best sex.

LUNAR ECLIPSE

We live with an awareness and an appreciation of the moon that is more pronounced, I think, than that which we feel for the sun. The longest period during which we who live in a temperate climate are separated from the sun is the length of the winter night. As interminable as that might sometimes seem, the breaking dawn always brings back the sun. Each morning, no matter how bleak, solar contact is renewed, and along with it, our sense of the sun as our constant companion. Perhaps because it is always present, we have come to take it for granted.

The moon, on the other hand, comes and goes, so that it seems less consistent, more erratic and elusive. Because the period of the moon's revolution around the earth and the period of rotation on its own axis are the same, it always presents the same face to us, even though it never looks the same from one night to the next. It departs daily in slender degrees, like slices cut from a voluptuous fruit, decreasing in size before our very eyes, eliciting a certain sadness as it shrinks. It changes its guise steadily, until finally disappearing altogether for three days at a time, after which it returns again in reversed increments, producing an exciting sensation of growing expectation along with its expanding girth.

The sun shines so brightly that it illuminates the entire world around us while at the same time rendering itself all but invisible by its very brightness. We can perceive the powerful presence of the sun in the ambient light it casts, but are only able to see the solar fire star itself through the filter of a cloud or a special lens. To look at its face directly is dangerous and painful. Plutarch remarked that "the effects of the moon are similar to the effects of reason and wisdom, whereas those of the sun appear to be brought about by physical force and violence."

Oddly, the ancients didn't necessarily associate the sun as the source of light. Genesis tells us that God created daylight before he did the sun and the moon. Many tribal peoples venerate the moon for its light-giving capacity. They consider moonlight to be more important, because it illuminates the night when it is more needed, whereas the sun only shines in the daytime when the sky is light already. Egyptians called the moon the Mother of the Universe, because the moon has, again according to Plutarch, "the light which makes moist and pregnant, is promotive of the generation of living beings and the fructification of plants." The Desana people of Colombia credit the "night sun" with promoting fertility through the production of light-giving dew.

The moon's light, reflecting the sun's as it does, is far less intense. We can stare at it, and do—some of us for hours at a time—without suffering the damaging effects of the sun. Of course, it is the indirect light of the sun that we see anyway when we look at the moon. A mirror image indelibly burned in the eye of the beholder. This is especially evident when the moon is full. The visage of that shimmering silver ball set in the vast blue sky and the lunar-lit atmosphere it creates has always held a universally mesmerizing, magnetic, mysterious, magical appeal.

Worship of the moon was pandemic and in most cultures preceded the more recent shift of allegiance to the sun. The status of the moon has always held precedence in Asia, and all religious occasions are still computed on a lunar calendar. Adam, according to Moses Maimonides, worshiped the moon, a religious holdover from Babylonian times. Even today, the most dapper, jaded urban dweller will take an instant, astonished notice of the full moon as if seeing it for the very first time. In so doing, she celebrates a simple celestial observance which connects her with the cosmos for a mystical moment. Ceremony at its most elemental.

> *Moon-soaked*
> *she emitted*
> *a cold radiance*
> *that made all*
> *who loved her*
> *leave her alone*
> *As well*
> *they might—*
> *silver track*

upmountain
to the moon.

Margaret Reckord
(Twentieth-century Jamaican)

People engage the moon in a most intimate and personalized relationship. We identify with it and make it our own. It is almost as though we can each hear it speak to us in a private language which only we can understand. The moon reflects not only the sun but our own earthly psyches as well. What child hasn't marveled that the moon follows her when she rides or walks at night?

Dogs, too, seem to notice this amazing phenomenon. What normally street-smart city-slicker pooch, my own dear Bud included, has not jumped at the sight of her own night shadow, moonstruck and suddenly skitterish at such proximity? What lonely lover, separated from the subject of her affections, does not take heart at the romantic revelation that the moon she sees is the same moon gazed upon, perhaps even simultaneously, by her distant love? These meaningful moon miracles have been discovered again and again by each new generation.

We are conscious of the circuits of the moon, and we relate them to our own internal cycles. Although the moon is almost a quarter of a million miles away, its influence is immense. When it is full, we experience an intensely potent psychological reaction, as if it were exerting the same pull on our emotions as it does on the waters that surround us. As Pliny, the Greek natural historian, noted, "The moon draws the sea after her with a powerful suction." So, too, are we sucked into an impressionable, unsettled, turbulent state of mind. Any firefighter, cop, teacher, or emergency room worker will be able to regale you with tales of the eccentric and/or violent behavior that occurs in coincidence with the full moon.

I cannot sleep
For the blaze of the full moon.
I thought I heard here and there
A voice calling.
Hopelessly I answer "Yes."
To the empty air.

Tzu Yeh
(Third-century Chinese)

Paracelsus, famed physician of the Middle Ages, considered the brain to be a "microcosmic moon" which responds to the full moon with increasing lunacy. Shakespeare had Othello say, "It is the very error of the moon, she comes more nearer earth than she was wont, and makes men mad." In 1842 Britain passed the Lunacy Act, which defined a lunatic as a deranged individual who was rational and lucid—that is, sane—during the dark and waxing phases of the moon, but "afflicted with a period of fatuity in the period following after the full moon."

The concept of moon madness is an old and widespread one, confirmed in language. Moon and mind and spiritual power are linked etymologically from the Indo-European precursor of both the Sanskrit *manas* and the Latin *mens*. From this root are derived the English words "menstruation," moon blood; "mania," moon madness; and "numinous," moon magic. The Roman moon goddess was called by two names, Luna and Mana. Her devotees, lunatics and maniacs, were condemned by the Christians as mad, crazy, or silly (which once meant "blessed"). The traditional forms of lunar worship were banned, and all things associated with the moon were held to be evil and wrong, having a detrimental effect on people, especially women, whose connection to the moon is biologically obvious.

Despite the dictates of the church, women continued to worship the moon all over Europe up through the Renaissance, when women knew that if they wanted something, they should pray not to God, but to the Lady Moon. This was especially true in Ireland and Iceland, where women sought the wisdom of the moon in sacred wells, and in some parts of those countries, they still do. Diana was the goddess of the crescent moon to the Druids. *Crescere* means "to grow," related to the Latin *creare*, "to create, to produce."

In her honor, women of Gaul baked crescent-shaped communion cakes to greet the rising of the new moon after three nights of dark skies. These are the same croissants that enjoy gustatory popularity today. Women in the Orient also bake moon cakes, round sweet rice balls to be enjoyed at the time of the Full Harvest Moon. Witches, practitioners of the old Wiccan religion, still convene on the full moon, at which time they ceremonially draw it down to earth for the purpose of creating positive magic.

> *From the darkness*
> *I go onto the road*
> *of darkness.*
> *Moon, shine on me from afar*
> *over the mountain edge.*
>
> Lady Izumi Shikibu
> (Tenth-century Japanese)

The presence of the moon stimulates our senses and activates our spirits, and its absence creates a feeling of foreboding. Cultures everywhere regard the phase of the moon when it is out of our sight as a precarious period during which we must exercise extreme care in all undertakings. Ranchers and farmers have long refrained from slaughtering, gelding, shearing, planting, and harvesting while the moon wanes from full to new for fear that the stock, the crops, would also wither and die.

The Babylonians neutralized the negative effects of these "black nights" by fasting and following a ritual program of propitiation. When people of the Gold Coast of Africa see the new moon, they throw ashes at it and say, "I saw you before you saw me." The first sighting of the waxing crescent moon still ushers in the new month throughout the Middle and Far East with a joyous, thankful celebration for its return to the heavens. If the monthly dark period of the moon affects us so deeply, so strongly, imagine the influence of an eclipse of the moon.

During the dark of a solar eclipse, people yield to a primal hysteria, horrified at the thought that once gone, the sun may never reappear and all would be lost. Prayers and rituals are employed to avert such a calamity. But because the process is relatively quick—the longest solar eclipses last a mere seven minutes or so—relief at the sun's inevitable return comes fairly soon. There is a recognizable beginning, middle, and end. The immediacy of a cosmic release and a satisfying sense of closure. Afterward, there is a sense of satisfaction which feels like what in a Hollywood movie would be leaning back and lighting up. Inhaling deeply. Aaaah.

An eclipse of the moon, including the partial phrases, is rather more subtle and a whole lot slower. The entire procedure takes a much longer time, and so the event seems less spectacular. And since you can actually look directly at its countenance without hurting your eyes, you can track the entire progression of light-to-dark-to-light. If you have the patience.

> *Ha go wa nab u na*
> *Ha go way nab u na* . . .
> We wait in the darkness!
> Come, all ye who listen,
> Help in our night journey:
> Now no sun is shining;
> Now no star is glowing;

Come show us the pathway:
The night is not friendly;
She closes her eyelids;
The moon has forgot us,
We wait in the darkness.

"Darkness Song"
Seneca Nation of the Iroquois League

I fell asleep once years ago during a lunar eclipse while sitting in the dark waiting for the moon to reappear. It was incredibly interesting and strangely sad to see the orbital moon appear to be slowly overtaken by the advancing shadow of the earth. But the dark stage was so long and the night was so late that sleep overcame me before the moon could return. This had a devastating effect on my psyche. All through the night I was troubled by angst-ridden dreams and I woke in the morning with an overwhelmingly unpleasant feeling of disquietude, of inner upheaval and darkness. I had witnessed the demise of the moon, and I felt bereft as if my best friend had died. It was days before I was able to shake my mournful mood.

In December 1992 I spent the duration of the period of totality of the lunar eclipse drumming in the dark with a small band of sturdy souls. Thanks to my favorite friendly astronomer at the Hayden Planetarium, I knew to the second the projected progression of the eclipse. The exact times of each stage. I knew precisely how long the moon would be dark. And yet, the longer we drummed, the more I rode the chanting, the more disturbed I got. Where the hell was the moon, anyway?

I found myself, head sweeping the sky like a rotating spotlight, absurdly, passionately looking for the missing moon in all the wrong places. I would spin around and around searching everywhere. Despite having witnessed six or seven other total lunar eclipses, quite a few partials, and the second longest total eclipse of the sun of this century; despite my rational knowledge and personal experience, here I was genuinely agitated in some extremely archetypal way.

> *o what will become of the world, the moon*
> *never dies without a cause*
> *only when a rich man is about to be*
> *killed*
> *is the moon murdered.*

Alsea moon eclipse exorcism

What if the moon didn't come back? (And where does it go, anyway?) What if, in our complacency, our stupidity, our cupidity, we have driven it away from us for good? A maddening thought.

Until, that is, it was verified by the aforementioned astronomer. When I described my experience, she said that she had a similar response to that same eclipse. It seems that normally when the moon is eclipsed, there remains a tinge, a hint, of dim red light, caused by the earth's shadow. A blood moon. But this eclipse was exceptionally dark, so that the moon became invisible not only to the naked eye but to the telescope as well. While she was trying to keep it in the site of her scope, she kept losing it. And she, too, scanned the sky desperately, looking for it. Searching blindly for our lost sister satellite. Scientist or no, she had succumbed to the same overwhelming, albeit irrational, fear.

What if the moon didn't come back?

> *Return soul of the sky, candid moon*
> *To the first sphere, shining and beautiful,*

And with your customary brilliance restore
The crown of silver to the darkened sky.

Chiara Cantarini Matraini
(Sixteenth-century Italian)

PART II

☆————————————————☾

Telling Time

ABOUT TIME

To think of time—of all that retrospection,
To think of to-day, and the ages continued henceforward.

Walt Whitman
(Nineteenth-century American)

I have recently emerged, immensely enriched and completely tranceformed, from an extended term of service in what I have come to think of as the hospice mode. During that excruciatingly intense time, I nursed neighbors, pets, friends, and family, many too many of my nearest and dearest relations, through adversity, disease, disaster, devastation, and death. A regular habitué of AIDS wards and emergency rooms, airports and waiting rooms, pharmacies and operating rooms, funeral parlors and cemeteries, I would joke that for years on end my only social life was conducted with people who were lying down. Except it was no joke.

Midwife and witness to the myriad transitional stages of death and dying, I found myself immersed in the drama and mundane detail, the minute-by-minute, day-to-day struggle of people dealing with a life-threatening disease. I did what I could in aid of their valiant determination to accept and prepare for their eventual demise, while at the same time (and often for the first time) investing themselves fully in the present. Together we endeavored to engage and embrace each precious moment one at a time until such time when our time will run out. Expire. And we with it. An invaluable lesson for us all when confronting the inevitable—whenever it might arise.

I observed at close range the ravages, the grave toll of time, the eternal taker. The grim reaper himself. That greedy sonofabastard robber baron so hell-bent on stealing my whole world away. Every time my mother would look at her body during her final frail few months, she would sigh with a profound sadness, "What happens to a person?" This was not a question, but a statement of actual, albeit poignant, fact, the emphasis resting on *happens*. I know precisely what she meant. Time, like gravity, *happens*. The recognition in corporeal terms that life itself, this particular life on earth, is quite terminal. In the end.

> *There is not a woman turns her face*
> *Upon a broken tree,*
> *And yet the beauties that I loved*

Are in my memory;
I spit into the face of Time
That has disfigured me.

W. B. Yeats
(Twentieth-century Irish)

During that seven-year eternity, I was Mama Donna by day, caring for my clan. At night, I would write my column. Research and read and ride my mind out onto the endless prairies, the panoramic sweep of time, of space, of species. Thoroughly entranced, I lost myself in the galloping exploration of the infinite vastness, the enormous distances, differences, durations, and dimensions of this marvelous macro/micro cosmos. The inconceivable magnificence of it all.

Night after night I would sit at my PC oracle, Sybil, pondering the perpetual round of universal order and the human condition: *Celestially Auspicious Occasions: Seasons, Cycles, and Celebrations.* Like Penelope, I spent my evenings in the dark, spinning cosmic yarns. Conjuring images, notes, and maps from my mental time travels into the eternal/temporal unknown, trying to interpret and trancelate what I had learned there. Some modicum of comprehension of the systematic interconnectivity, the intricate complexity, the enduring continuity of That Which Is.

My daytime duties and nighttime ruminations resulted in an oddly juxtaposed notion of time. On the one hand, I could clearly see that there is truth in those old truisms. Time does, indeed, march on. *Tempus* certainly *fugits* and it stops for absolutely no one. My personal, practical experience of the transitory nature of physical time led me to perceive its passing as a destructive force devouring everything in its path. Another day older and deeper in debt. But this view was tempered by my writing and ritual practice. Conducted in sacred time, this work kept me connected with the cosmos, my soul in contact with the creative and generative qualities of time beyond fathomed time. And here I found consolation. Time really does heal all wounds.

Time's violence rends the soul; by the rent eternity enters.

Simone Weil, *Gravity and Grace*
(Twentieth-century French)

Time is a paradox, at once temporary and permanent, external and internal, objective and subjective. Time flies and time stands still. Time passes, but is forever. Time is like a river, flowing, irreversible, ever onward. Time is like an arrow aimed directly at the future far in the distance. It is also like a wheel turning, returning, and turning again. Or like a snake biting its own tail, propelling itself along, rolling like a hoop down a hill. Time creates. Time maintains. Time destroys. We save time, we waste time, we keep time, we lose time, we kill time, we make time, we take time out.

Time is at once universal and intensely personal. It surrounds us and is, at the same time, deep within us. Its surging rhythmic force moves the entire world and us as well. The throbbing tempo of the universe reverberates in each beat of our heart. Its clear cadence, the repeated patterns of light and dark, warm and cold, wet and dry, high tide and low, growth and death, yin and yang, evident in the natural order, is echoed in our own bodies, our biorhythms, our blood. Our internally alternating cycles of activity and rest, energy and mood, sleep and dream, hunger and hormone. The oscillating pulse of the planets surges through our veins and we vibrate in time with the stars.

Duplicitous in its definitions, time can be said to describe a series of moments, each unique, distinct, and countable. Each lustrous, like a pearl. Each pearl, the eternal present. For the ancient Greeks, the moment was enough. Their perception of *cosmos*, the universal working order, was rooted in the reality of time, the moment, as life itself. Be here now. The Hopis, like many tribal peoples, do not perceive time in terms of before/after, earlier/later, yesterday, today, and tomorrow. Their language is not divided into past, present, and future tenses, but into states of manifestation: imagined/real, abstract/concrete, intended/actualized. For them, time is not a flowing entity, but the constant staccato repetition of the same event over and over again, each time with subtle shadings. According to this construct, each generation of occurrence affects the next, rather like the movie *Ground Hog Day*.

The great religions of Western civilization—Zoroastrianism, Judaism, Christianity, and Islam—share the basic precept that time is linear, like beads strung in unending succession on a cord that reaches to eternity. The concept of linear time signifies evolution, development, progress; implies destiny, salvation. Starting with the Old Testament, time is the compilation in chronological order of the sequence of accumulative historic events through which the master plan of God's purpose unfolds. This view of the process of the unfolding of time is like the gradual rolling out of an enormous, ornate Oriental carpet in order to expose its mystifyingly complex pattern. For the Christian world, time is an epic poem divided into two books: Part I, B.C., "Before Christ"; Part II, A.D., "*Anno Domini*, In the Year of the Lord."

But by far the more prevalent viewpoint through the ages, as expressed in some forms of Gnosticism, Hinduism, Buddhism, Orphism, and other indigenous and Oriental philosophies, regards time as continuous and circular, as if the ends of the string of pearls had been cleverly joined to reveal no beginning and no end. This divine necklace is then worn wrapped many times around the throat, encircling all existence in the sinuous spiral of the never-ending cycles of time. Buddhists conceive of time as perpetually recycling itself in an eternally repetitive pattern. Circular time represents the enduring essence of ever-regenerating, omnipresent energy, with little importance placed on the distinction between past and future.

Modern Hindustani illustrates a linguistic example of this same conceptual indifference. *Kal* means both "yesterday" and "tomorrow"; *parson* means "the day before tomorrow" as well as "the day after tomorrow"; and *atarson* means "three days ago" and "three days from now." For Hindus, time refers to continuously recurring cycles of ages, called *yugas*, each of which is divided into four parts: a million-year-long golden age, a silver age, a bronze age, and an iron age, the shortest, which lasts upwards of 400,000 years—the current age in which we live. These repeating periods of time alternate between divine creation and dissolution, dissolution and creation. Life and death, the constant transmigration of souls, follow this same course, riding the reincarnation wheel of fortune through fate and time, time and time again.

> *The singer of this liberating song*
>   *laughs loud and long:*
> "*We will be in the end*
>   *what we were in the beginning,*
> *clear bubbles forming and dissolving*
>   *in the stream of timeless Mother Wisdom.*"

> Lex Hixon/Ramprasad
> (Twentieth-century American,
> eighteenth-century Bengali)

Time also defines duration. Like an accounting of the carats in each pearl, it is the measurement of the span of a single happening, a particular moment in time. An era, an epoch, an age, a period, a millennium, a century, a decade, a year, a quarter, a month, a fortnight, a week, a day, a morning, an hour, a half hour, a minute, a second, a millisecond, a microsecond, a nanosecond, a picosecond, a femtosecond. Or duration can refer to the amount of time that has lapsed between events, the interval, which is like the carefully executed knot that separates each bead on the necklace. Duration expressed as time is absolute enough to measure with astonishing precision, and yet it remains completely relative. Time, like space, like beauty, is totally in the eye of the beholder. As Einstein said, "When you sit with a pretty girl for two hours, you think it's only a minute. But when you sit on a hot stove for a minute, you think it's two hours."

How long is time? How old? When did it begin? Who knows? Our universe is thought to be some 10 to 20 billion years old. The earth, a young adult planet in cosmic terms, is barely 4.5 billion years old. Imagine a ratio wherein the span of the life of the world is equal to one year. Earth was born on January 1, New Year's Day. A few weeks later, it had cooled and congealed enough to form a rocky crust, but it wasn't until August, some 2 billion years ago, that terrestrial conditions became conducive to the development of life. By the end of October, the planet was teeming with living things, mostly aquatic. The dinosaurs reigned during mid-December. The first mammals showed up in time for the Winter Solstice.

Then, at 11:55 P.M. on December 31, New Year's Eve, human beings, the new kids on the block, wandered onto the scene blowing their whistles and tooting their horns. People have been around for an equivalent of five minutes of the whole year. The length of recorded history is about as long as the clock tower bell takes to strike midnight. Twelve seconds. Which makes the life span of an individual person, what? As long as the blink of an eye? Whose eye? An elephant's or a mosquito's?

I have read that *Homo sapiens* are the only time-conscious species, but I can't quite buy that, having seen a dog bury several bones in several locations and then dig them all up again months later. Don't tell me she wasn't intentionally salting away a little something for a rainy day. She might have been a mutt, but she was no fool. She saved in preparation for her future.

I *will* concede, however, that human beings *do* display a singularly enthusiastic interest in time. An especially acute and astute awareness. Actually, we are completely obsessed. It is this peculiar bit of genetic programming that has set us apart. Animals and plants react automatically to light fluctuations, temperature swings, and seasonal changes out of an inbred instinct, some preprogrammed, indelibly imprinted time-sense. Our ancestors, on the other hand, had to figure it out for themselves. And they had to be right.

It was the conscious act of taking possession of time that elevated people into a realm separate from that of the animals. Before humans acquired time, Tsimshian Indians believe, men and women were still like the animals. Before we knew time, people could still marry the moon, say the Aleuts. The Bambaras, the Sulkas, and the natives of Vanuatu maintain that the communication channels that once linked earth and heaven were still open before the taking of time. The Egyptians claimed that before time, the god/desses were not yet born.

A more clearly defined shape of nature came with time. With time came the deities of Egypt. Light came with the dawn of time, agree the tribes of Tlingit, Vanuatu, and biblical Israel. The Luiseños, Pomos, and Aleuts relate that the beginning of time caused the moon to rise and begin on its course of changing ways. The belief that the advent of time was accompanied by the coming into existence of all living things is also quite widespread.

From our earliest beginnings, people have paid exquisite attention to time and its telling; its manifestations and ramifications. On the material level, this capacity to reckon time in terms of consequence, to observe, reason, and draw conclusions, has allowed humanity to adapt successfully to an environment of less-than-certain circumstances. Humankind's faculty for memory and expectation is evidenced by the ability to apply past experience to action employed in the present in order to plan for the future. This made it possible for people to make ample provision for their current and anticipated needs: to create and carry out the design of an implement, a garment, a ritual, or a structure; to make a tool or a strategy; to acquire a culture.

While our fixation on time has been fundamental in ensuring the survival of the species, it has also rendered us pitifully insecure in the face of our understanding of our own mortality. With our expanded sense of time-consciousness, we could easily, if not comfortably, suppose a future without us in it. The more we understand of the universal patterns and perspectives of time, the more we realize what a minuscule role we play in the overall scheme.

In order to comfort ourselves and help us cope, people have devised all sorts of belief systems—symbolism, spirituality, philosophy, religion, science, and superstition—to address our endless questions concerning time after death and existence beyond time. Primal fear of the unknown has propelled us to forge an alliance with time, to enlist its support on our behalf. We needed to domesticate it to serve our personal and societal purposes. Measure it, count it, split it into useful units. Mold it to the specifications of our unique life and times.

Searching for assurance that time is, after all, on our side, our foreparents scoped the heavens for clues with which to solve the mystery of their own existence. Hitching their wagons to the turning wheel of time, they established their societies in imitation, in cooperation, and in honor of the immutable laws of the universe.

They invariably set apart sacred time in which to acknowledge their identification with the eternal cyclical order of seasons and changes. In this time out of time, they communed with the deities and the spiritual energies of nature and synchronized their pulses with the ticking mechanism of the universe. With the observation, the celebration, of sacred time comes the recognition that one's role, though undeniably, undauntingly tiny, is not insignificant, but a perfectly fitted piece intrinsic to the completion of the puzzle.

We modern folk who live our lives completely encased in cocoons spun of artificial environments and arbitrary measures have developed a foreshortened viewpoint of time. Our well-honed concepts of time have become clouded by dictatorial external schedules, conceived, not in accordance with universal time, nor necessarily even for our benefit, but as some well-oiled contrivance designed for the smooth functioning of international communication, commerce, and sporting competitions. We have come to think in terms of school year, workweek, weekend, business day, banker's hours, split seconds. Our always advancing manipulations of time have undoubtedly made our communal lives more manageable, but have wreaked havoc with our understanding of everlasting sacred time. Our vision has dimmed.

We tend to conceptualize time in terms of the span of a human lifetime—specifically our own. Our definition of permanence is that which lasts longer than we do—stone, for example, or steel, although I have seen statues of saints that have had their marble or bronze extremities kissed away by centuries-long streams of puckered devotees. Our insular perspective is no less ludicrous than that famous Steinberg *New Yorker* magazine cover showing a map of the United States drawn from the point of view of New York City. Manhattan in the foreground is in fine detail. The Hudson River just to the west is clear enough. And there on the other side, vaguely recognizable, an uninteresting, ignorant blur, lies the rest of the country. Like time and space. Out there. Somewhere . . .

It is particularly difficult for us of the urban persuasion, divorced as we have become from the eternal truths of time, to picture ourselves as part of the grand cosmic design. We have forgotten our once vital role as active participants, partners even, in this intricately interconnected and interdependent universe of ours. And, as a result, we have suffered a spiritual disconnection which places us smack back to our quaking beginnings.

It is possible to believe that all the past is but the beginning of a beginning, and that all that is and has been is but the twilight of the dawn. It is possible to believe that all that the human mind has ever accomplished is but the dream before the awakening.

H. G. Wells, "The Discovery of the Future"
(Twentieth-century English)

THE DAY

So teach us to number our days
That we may get us a heart of wisdom.

Psalms 90:12

It takes a certain amount of knowledge—specific, sophisticated astronomical, geographical, and mathematical information and experience—plus a well-planned, purposeful, and assiduous attention to the skies to be able to determine the beginning and end points, the precise length, of a year or a month. There are, therefore, great discrepancies from culture to culture as to how these are counted, their sequence and cycles described. Solar years; lunar years; lunar/solar years; years that are assigned to the ascent of a certain star, constellation, planet; the harvest of a particular plant; the rising of a river. Lunar months; solar/lunar months; mathematical, creative, calendrical weeks and months of varied definitions and durations.

It is all but impossible, however, not to notice and recognize the daily oscillation of light and dark, dark and light. This rhythm provides us with the parameters of the prime unit of time, nature's most basic, immediate, and personal period. Day and night are the first experience of changing time that young children can relate to. When she was four, the only way my fairy goddess daughter was able to conceive or express the passage of time was "when it gets dark" or "when it gets light." This could equally stand for "earlier," "later," "before," "after," "yesterday," "tomorrow," "this morning," "next week," or "last year."

For the Mayans, "sun" and "time" were the same substance and were represented by the same glyph, called *kin*. The only differences in the delineation of a day among societies arise insofar as pinpointing when the day begins and ends and how it is divided.

Most peoples through time have understandably considered the start of a new day to be sunrise, dawn being such a powerful symbol of resurrection and regeneration. "Plan your life at New Year and your day at dawn," instructs the traditional Japanese proverb. For the Mekeo people of Papua New Guinea, the dawn bird sings up the start of the day. In Mexico, innumerable cocks crow the morning into session. The Sioux say that the day breaks when a horse neighs. The day ends when the sun sets.

One of my better childhood memories was singing Taps at Girl Scout camp.

> *Day is done.*
> *Gone the sun.*
> *From the lakes,*
> *From the hills,*
> *From the sky.*
> *All is well,*
> *Safely rest.*
> *God is nigh.*

Some, notably Jews and Muslims, commence a day at sunset, envisioning the darkness as the inception of the light. Day began in medieval Basel at noon, but it was called one o'clock. The start of the contemporary secular calendar day is counted at precisely one minute past midnight, a completely arbitrary time which bears reference to absolutely nothing in nature, but is convenient for record keeping, coordination, and regulation.

For many millennia it was enough to distinguish day from night. There was no great need for hunters and gatherers to organize their efforts in a precisely timed fashion. Living, as they did (and still do in some few places), according to circumstance, happenstance, and the unpredictable vagaries of life, one day, one night, was sufficient unto itself. It was helpful, though, at the very least, to know which roots and herbs were best to pick for succulence and potency at dusk and dawn. These two divisions of day, morning and night, are the only ones mentioned by the early Greek writers Homer and Hesiod.

In settled agricultural communities, divisions of a day were only meaningful in terms of prescribing common actions to be undertaken at certain times every day. Milking time, market time, meal time, pasturing time, times for prayer and assembly. The Zend-Avesta tells us that the ancient Persians identified five distinct daily periods: Dawn, from midnight to sunrise; the Time of Sacrifice, from sunrise to midday; the Time of Full Light, from noon to sunset; the Rising of the Stars, from sunset until the stars appeared; and the Time of Prayer, from starshine to midnight. Nights, during which nothing happened, were not specifically noted. The Romans, many centuries later, marked seven sections of the day. In early Britain, the day was sectioned into four "tides."

Time periods were most often indicated by concrete phenomena, for example the exact position of the sun in relationship to the earth, from the human vantage point. The time could be shown simply by pointing to the site occupied by the sun in the sky at the moment in question. The Konso people of Central Africa, who still refer to the time by pointing to the sun's station, divide the daylight hours into seven unequal periods, each with its associated activities. Early hours are long to reflect the slower pace dictated by the heat. Because the sun sits directly overhead at high noon, it is best avoided by all but "mad dogs and Englishmen." Many tasks, then, need to be accomplished in the relative cool of the late afternoon and evening, hence the shorter duration of each hour.

As agricultural-based societies became more complex, it was important to institutionalize public time. This was less in the interest of improving its accuracy than as a socioreligious organizational device employed by the highly developed city-states of Europe, North Africa, and Mesoamerica. When he saw the sun slide between the Rostrum and the Grecostais, two prominent buildings in the ancient Forum, the official Roman timekeeper shouted out the noon hour. Across the Atlantic, the same scene was enacted by his Aztec counterpart, who also announced from the plaza at the Templo Mayor in Tenochtitlán (Mexico City) the times of the opening and closing of the market, the beginning of games, and the proper hours for worship.

In much the same way, time was regulated during the European Middle Ages by work clocks. Essentially public address systems, these were a complicated combination of bells of varying pitch rung in specific order at intervals of diverse duration. Each distinct toll announced the times that concerned the entire citizenry: when to begin and end work, the daily market hours, assorted calls to assembly, and the beginning and end of nightly curfews. The town criers in colonial North America served the same function. Like news radio, they kept up a running commentary on the events of the day, the weather, and a constant reminder of the time.

The Acadians of ancient Chaldea were the first to subdivide the day, as well as the year, into equal parts. In the same way that their year counted twelve months of thirty days each, their day comprised twelve *danna*, the equivalent of two modern hours, which in turn were divided into thirty *ges*, each four minutes long. It was the Egyptians who first developed a twenty-four-hour day, most likely for religious reasons. Time was enumerated in order to arrange for the performance of particular rituals. The Egyptian word for "hour," *wnwt*, also means "priestly duties." By extension, *wnwty* refers to an "hour-watcher" as well as a "star-watcher." The Christian Church in the period of the Roman Empire had formalized and expanded the biblical practice of praying three times each day, in the morning, in midafternoon, and at night.

Hours designated to regulate periods of activity and rest could be told by referring to the sun's reflection on the earth by means of a *gnomen*, "one that knows," a post stuck into the ground. The approximate hourly time was told by noting the angle of the shadow cast by the post on an inscribed numbered scale as the day progressed. Variations on this simple sundial were the principle timekeeping device for over four thousand years, from their invention in ancient Egypt until the sixteenth century. The *Hsin Lun*, or *New Discourses*, written in A.D. 550 by

Liu Hsieh, includes a chapter called "Sparing Time," which states that "the worthies of old, wishing to spread abroad benevolence and righteousness in the world, were always struggling against time. They set no value on whole foot-lengths of jade, but a tenth of an inch of shadow [on a sundial] was as precious as pearls to them."

These shadow clocks, of course, weren't quite so effective when the sky was overcast. The author of an Egyptian document written in the second century B.C. might have been referring to an eclipse when s/he wrote, "One cannot tell when it is midday, one cannot record the shadows." The Egyptians also developed water clocks, clepsydrae, for use at night. These instruments were revolutionary in that, in addition to telling each hour, they made visible, and thus comprehendable for the first time, the number of hours that had transpired in a given period. Water clocks measured the flow of time, inspired, no doubt, by philosophical concepts that likened time to a flowing river, a continuously moving stream. A crude sort of water clock was used in the Senate and law courts in both classical Greece and Rome in order to limit the time allotted to long-winded orators.

A cross-cultural panoply of creative time-telling devices based on the same notion of movement have been constructed over the ages. These ingenious systems were all operated by a carefully controlled inflow or outflow of some substance, causing it to run from one marked receptacle to another. Sand, oil, mercury, and stone pellets, in addition to water, have been utilized. Fire, too, has been employed to cause the combustion of an oil or candle wick which ran along a marked track. The most common clock in use in China ran on incense. The powder was poured into a pattern of carved grooves and then ignited. As it burned, it meandered along, like lazy time on a warm summer day.

The remarkable grandmother of all timepieces was constructed in Fez, Morocco, in A.D. 1357. The thirty-seven-foot-long structure held a room-sized water clock which activated a mechanism that released a hail of pebbles. The pebbles rolled down wooden spouts sticking out from under the roof and fell onto gongs set at intervals twenty feet below, creating a clamorous din. At the same time, one of the twelve doors located under a line of arches embedded halfway down the front facade would burst open, revealing which hour had been struck. This door remained ajar until the following cacophonous hour was struck, at which point it shut as the next door in the row opened in turn.

> *Minutes, like rivers, shake*
> *the city walls, each house, each gate.*
>
> Annette Elisabeth von Droste-Hülshoff
> (Nineteenth-century German)

No matter how clever or complex these devices were, they could never be truly accurate. Flow clocks, for example, which run by gravity, start out at a faster pace, and then as the feeder container empties and the pressure drops, time slows way down. Sundials and shadow clocks depend on the sun, which is sometimes obsured by clouds. Seasonal changes cause a difference in the length of day and night. Depending on latitude, the correct time according to the sun changes by one minute for each fourteen miles traveled in an east-west direction. Quirky planetary orbits also vary in pace, hurrying up and slowing down from time to time, making some days longer than others by seconds and minutes.

Once the demands of increased production and organized trade dictated that "time is money," it became imperative to be able to count time as carefully as gold. What was needed was a system of mechanical timekeeping that did not depend on nature, which is, after all, thoroughly capricious and notoriously undependable. Clocks and calendars were called for which, because they were independent, artificial, and abstract, were guaranteed of being reliable, exactly uniform, and unchanging.

Western civilization and its science were faced with a choice. We could stay married to the sun and suffer sloppy bookkeeping, or we could divorce it for the sake of exquisitely correct clocks. Business is business, after all, so the *apparent* sun was thus banished and replaced with the *mean* sun, an idealized, hypothetical, wholly fictional character.

His notebooks of 1480–90 show that Leonardo da Vinci understood the motion of pendulums, and he put them to creative use. It was Galileo, the seventeenth-century grand master mechanic, who conceived of a pendulum-based clock. It is ironic that Galileo, who had been condemned by the church for heresy for announcing that the earth orbited around the sun and not the other way around, was the first to successfully separate the day from the sun. He died without having actually built the clock, but he passed the design on to his son Vicenzo, who hadn't completed it either by the time of his death seven years later in 1649. Eventually, the Duke of Tuscany commissioned its manufacture by Philip Treffler of Germany, and with it the birth of a truly new world order.

She knew they needed a clock. But she could not work with it going every second. When it was going every second that way, she could not seem to take her eyes off of it, and because it made no noise she found herself making the noise for it in her mind.

Joan Didion, *Run River*
(Twentieth-century American)

The ages of discovery, exploration, and colonization and the concomitant opportunities for ever-expanding trade routes and commerce required, in addition to accuracy, a unified standard-ization of time. Timekeeping, until barely a hundred years ago, was an entirely local affair. Until the twentieth century, every harbor town of any size would drop a time ball from a tall tower at noon each day. Captains at sea could then adjust their chro-nometers to local time. Today billions of synchronized people worldwide set their clocks and their resolutions to the start of a new year when at midnight the great lighted ball falls on Times Square in New York City.

Clocks, though separately accurate for their particular lon-gitude, registered very different times from city to city across continents. Travelers needed extensive time conversion tables to be able to cope and had to adjust their pocket clocks con-stantly to stay current. As late as 1882, there were over one hundred local railroad times. A typical train trip from Maine to California necessitated twenty time changes from coast to coast. One passenger, Charles Ferdinand Dowd, possessed of a par-ticularly meticulous disposition, was outraged at the confusion caused by such lackadaisical timekeeping. In 1869 he devised a zone system whereby the continent would be divided into four geographical bands, each fifteen degrees of longitude wide and stretching from pole to pole. All sections would share a uniform time in minutes and seconds; only the hour would vary from one zone to another. After fourteen years of persistent lobby-ing, the railroads finally instituted standard time at twelve o'clock noon, Sunday, November 18, 1883. According to *Har-per's Weekly*, ". . . no clock struck for this hour until the sun reached the 75th meridian. Then all the clocks on the continent struck together, those in the Eastern Belt striking 12; the Cen-tral belt 11, in the Mountain Belt 10 and in the Pacific Belt 9." International standard time followed the next year.

The more we try to tame time, to mold it and shape it to our own unnatural needs, the faster it seems to flee. And the older we get, the more aware we are of its headlong rush away from us. Our aging biological clocks beat out the years in an increasingly rapid cadence. There have been, I can assure you, many moments this year—the culmination of my first fifty years (this time) on earth—during which I have paused, in midstep, in utter panic, to realize just how many more I might realistically still expect. Fifty! My grandmother and mother each lived for eighty years. That's thirty more, *más o menos*. The same period, exactly, as my entire adult life span. Three decades during which *a lot* happened. But still and all, thirty years passed in a snap.

> *There are thirty-six thousand days*
> *to a life*
> *And I have wasted sixteen*
> *thousand*
> *on nothing.*
> *Please tell God to set back his*
> *clock.*
>
> Nguyen Cong Tru
> (Eighteenth-century Vietnamese)

A day can be a very long time. 1,440 minutes. 86,400 seconds. In the space of one day's time, the earth makes a complete rotation on its axis, a round-trip, as it were, of some 25,000 miles at the equator. In the course of our continuous journey, over one thousand pounds of cosmic matter enter our atmosphere and reach the earth each day. Ten thousand American babies are born each day. Seven hours is about how much time the average American wastes by watching television each day.

We blink our eyes over 10,000 times a day. We take a breath fifteen times a minute, or in excess of 21,500 times per diem. In one day, each of us processes 3,600 gallons of air. And Americans collectively pass more than 9 million cubic feet of gas each day. That is enough to inflate a balloon with a diameter of 250 feet. We filter 10 billion gallons of liquid through our kidneys, enough to fill 500 million kidney-shaped swimming pools. Together we grow six square miles of new skin.

Our hearts beat around 72 times a minute, 4,320 times a day, pumping 70 gallons of blood. Every day 8,400 people suffer heart attacks, 1,500 of which are fatal. All the hearts in the United States collectively pump 400 billion gallons daily, enough to fill the deep and wide Mississippi River at Vicksburg. All of our hearts together generate enough energy, 8 million kilowatts, to run 150 locomotives for twenty-four hours.

Just think what we could do with all that heart power.

THE WEEK

Implicit in each new week, as in any new beginning, is the reminder that "today is the first day of the rest of your life." It's a fresh start, another chance for a change. A week is such a manageable amount of time, so strangely satisfying. Longer than a day, which is always too short; shorter than a month, which is too long to take hold of, keep track of, to grasp. A week, neatly self-contained unit that it is, is a perfectly reasonable period of time in which to establish and accomplish short-term goals, schedule repetitive tasks, and arrange for obligations, engagements, appointments, enlightenments, and entertainments.

The week is a totally arbitrary unit, more subject to personal and societal interpretation than any other measure of time. The week varies considerably in length from culture to culture, but however long, any particular week always has the same mutually agreed-upon number of days. Unlike the month and year, its length is constant, never changing, always starting at the same time and on the same day. The week is also different from the day, the month, and the year in that it has no natural correspondence with the cycles of the universe.

The day is determined by the twenty-four-hour cycle of alternating sun and shadow that results from the rotation of the earth on its axis. This duration governs our own daily round of basic maintenance—when we move around and rest, eat and drink, sleep and dream, poop and pee; our body rhythms and chemistry. The month relates to the cyclical movements of the moon as it orbits the earth. Because the changes in its countenance are so graphically obvious, the moon is easy to track. The year, as we count it, charts the earth's revolution around the sun. The week alone is an artificial arithmetic organization of time, which establishes a consistently recurring rhythm of days.

A weekly division of time arose with the market economy as a structure to coordinate commerce. Dependent on trade for survival, isolated agricultural communities arranged to meet every so many days at such and such a village in order to engage in the regular exchange of goods and services as well as to provide opportunities for meeting, news gathering, socializing, worshiping, courting, gaming, and all sorts of diversions and indulgences.

Market day was too important and enjoyable to miss. Since

settlements were generally spaced a good distance apart and travel was most likely by foot, one would want to know exactly when and where to go for what. Hence the development of the market week system with its rotating schedule of regional trade fairs, which still predominates in many parts of the developing world today, where every cognoscente knows which day which village hosts which market with which specialties. In much the same way, cosmopolitan shopping aficionados keep mental track of the weekly circuits of street fairs, farmers' markets, flea markets, antique shows, yard sales, and the daily hours of stores and malls, the modern equivalents.

The idea of market and the idea of week are merged etymologically in several West African languages. *Kasoa* in Tiv and *urua* in Efik mean both "week" and "market," as does the Indonesian *pasar*, and in all cases they are used interchangeably. The Ewes and the Yorubas name the days of the week "market day," "second day of the market," "market day is tomorrow." The Yoruba people practice a sixteen-day market cycle, which is subdivided into four four-day weeks. The four-day market week reigns supreme throughout most of West Africa, East Africa, and along the lower Congo. Until only decades ago, market weeks of three, five, six, nine, and ten days were popular in Rwanda, Tanzania, Cameroon, Togo, and Zaire and are still observed in parts of Ghana, Nigeria, and Burkina Faso (Upper Volta).

In ancient Colombia and New Guinea, market weeks were comprised of three days. The old Germanic tribes as well as those in pre-Columbian Mesoamerica and Indochina counted a week as five days. In Assyria the weekly cycle was six days, in ancient Egypt it was ten days, and in China it was a complex twelve-day week comprised of combinations of three- and six-day market week cycles. The Incas used an eight-day week. At each week's end, the king changed wives. By the eighth century B.C., several Italian cultures had evolved a periodic schedule of eight intervening days between markets, the ninth being market day.

Rome inherited this system of eight-day market weeks from the Etruscans, and for seven or eight centuries, the *nundinae*, or "ninth-day affairs," ruled not only the economy but the associated social and political community life as well. On market day, schools and courts were closed, public meetings suspended, and all work stopped. Baths and banquets were frequented. The seven-day week was introduced by the Christians to Rome, where it rivaled the traditionally held eight-day week. For a time, the two were used simultaneously, but eventually, the seven-day week proved more popular. It was officially adopted by Constantine, emperor of Rome, A.D. 321 and carried to the far corners of the empire.

Inherent in the concept of a week, however it is tabulated, is a consistent cadence of work time offset by regular rest time. The weekly beat is measured by a periodic time-off, which punctuates the mundane workweek and becomes its high point. The TGIF weekend. Market day with its festive atmosphere, holiday spirit, and sensory overload was usually the centerpiece around which the week revolved. The idea of a special day each week during which we allow ourselves a change of activity, of pace, of focus, from the ordinary toil it takes to survive is a distinctly agricultural one.

Herding and hunting cultures have less need for regulated rest time. Pastoral peoples spend vast amounts of leisure time while they sit back and watch the sheep, reindeer, cows, and goats graze. Hunters and gatherers don't work until they have to. They enjoy the bounty of what they collect or kill until the cache runs out, at which point they make a foray for some more.

Farming, however, is "women's work" writ large. Extended domestic upkeep on a grand scale. Mothering Mother Nature. Planting, tending, nurturing, nursing. A never-ending and exhausting series of chores. Always alert and on call. A sabbath as a rest day was deemed so necessary by the agrarian communities in the area of the Fertile Crescent that its observance was extended to the land of the fields, which were allowed to lie fallow for one year in every seven.

The week of seven days, first developed by Babylonian astronomer/astrologers, spread and took hold throughout the Middle East and was firmly established there before biblical times. While it is commonly assumed that the customary Judeo-Christian-Islamic seven-day week came about in imitation of the Hebrew god, who is said to have created the world in six days and rested on the seventh, it is much more probable that Yahweh's work and rest schedule was adapted to the seven-day workweek/weekend sabbath cycle already followed by his worshipers.

The heaven and earth were finished, and all their array. On the seventh day God finished the work that he had been doing, and he ceased on the seventh day from all the work he had done.

Genesis 2:2

Yahweh was actually the last in a line of Middle Eastern patriarchal gods who worked for six days to birth the heavens and earth and then took a day off from their labors. Ahura-Mazda of Persia, Ptah of Memphis, Marduk of Babylonia, and Baal of Syria all did the same before him. The inspiration for this seven-day work/rest sequence can be traced back to worship of the Hindu goddess Durga, the impassioned warrior-mother who fights to protect her children. It was the custom for Indian women who had given birth to complete a week-long ceremony of safekeeping for their newborns. On the sixth day of casting continuous spells, they would invoke the energy of Durga in her aspect of Shasti, "the sixth," the Leader of the

Mothers. Thus completing the obligatory ritual week, she rested on the seventh day before resuming her normal life.

The seven-day week, as it was ultimately adopted by the Egyptians, Romans, Hebrews, Christians, Muslims, and Hindus, is now the globally accepted standard for commercial, cultural, and political exchange. But why, when a week of any multiple of days would do as well, was it that the seven-day week was the one to take hold? Why seven? What special resonance did/does it have for so many for so long? Could it be that the week as we know it reflects the cosmic swing of the celestial spheres after all?

The moon exhibits four distinctly different faces each time it makes its round every twenty-nine and a half days. Four phases of the moon, four weeks of the month. The week of the new, the waxing crescent, the full, and the waning crescent moon. A moon dance in four/four time, the tempo of transformation. Babylonians and Assyrians observed a lunar sabbath at each turn of the cycle, every seven days or so. They refrained from work on these auspicious days, as all endeavor was considered to be unlucky at the times of the changes of the moon. Buddhists observe an *Uposatha* four times each lunar month. During these sabbaths on the days of the new and full moon and the two quarter-moons, people commonly fast and cease all secular activities in otherworldly reverence.

That the lunar sabbath tradition was still strong among the biblical Hebrews is evident in the origins of the word "sabbath." The Hebrew *shabbat* comes originally from the Semitic Akkadian *shapatu*, meaning "the night of the full moon." *Shabbat* may also be related to the Moorish *zabat*, an "occasion of power." Zabats are still celebrated by Berber women, the rumored North African descendants of the Amazons, who dance in groups of thirteen for the thirteen annual lunations. Sabbats, Wiccan ceremonial festivals, are traditionally celebrated in covens of thirteen witches.

As monotheists, the early Jews were most anxious to separate the notion of God, an ideal supranatural force, from the image of any natural element and themselves from any taint of pagan practice: earth, sky, moon, animal, idol, goddess, nature worship. Jews are enjoined in several biblical passages to observe and keep holy the sabbath ordained and blessed by God. This day of rest, dedicated to prayer and family ceremony, was to be celebrated every seven days regardless of the moon's course—a completely revolutionary and creative concept. By rounding off the true lunar quarter, a week of seven days and nine hours, they successfully drove a wedge into the natural symmetry of time. Thus divorced, the week went out of sync with the moon in only a matter of months. And so the week stands alone, an abstract artistic structure for the theological message of the oneness of God.

The Hellenistic seven-day week was essentially astrological, linked to the stars, an amalgam of the astronomy, astrology, and math of the great scientific cultures of Egypt, Mesopotamia, and Greece. The days of the week were associated with those moving heavenly bodies that were visible with the naked eye: the sun, the moon, Mars, Mercury, Jupiter, Venus, and Saturn. The cultural and mythological importance of the seven planets, and, incidentally, the seven colors of the spectrum and seven notes on the musical scale, was so strong that the number seven has enjoyed a lasting reputation as being lucky.

The days of the week were named for the planets. The Day of Saturn, for instance. The Day of the Sun. The Moon's Day. *Dies saturni, dies solis, dies lunae,* in Latin. Saturday, Sunday, Monday. The English weekdays come from the Anglo-Saxon translations of the planets as well as the god/desses in whose honor they were dedicated. The northern equivalent of Mars, the war god, is the warrior Tyr (Tuesday); Mercury's counterpart was Odin or Woden, also a messenger god (Wednesday); Jupiter was Donar/Thunar/Thor, the supreme deity (Thursday); and Venus' Day went to the love goddess Frigg/Fria (Friday).

The Christian Church refused to acknowledge this pagan terminology and continued to refer to the days solely by numbers: "weekday II," "weekday III," and so forth. The sabbath alone had a name, the Lord's Day, *dies domenica*, which is reflected in the name for Sunday in modern Latin languages: *domingo* in Spanish and Portuguese, *dimanche* in French, *domenica* in Italian, and *duminicā* in Romanian. The weekdays are still numbered in modern Portuguese: *segundo-feira, têrça-feira*. The Quakers still refer to Sunday as First Day.

The English word "week" comes from the Old Norse *vikja,* "to turn." And, according to some biologists, our systems seem to fluctuate as the week turns its somersaults within us as well. Modern chronobiology has identified a seven-day biorhythm cycle in certain human biochemical responses. We experience small variations in blood pressure, heartbeat, and response to infection on a weekly basis. And it is at intervals of one week that the body's rejection of transplanted organs usually peaks. Perhaps thousands of years of relating to a seven-day week that includes cycles of work and rest might have had a subliminal effect on these automatic internal changes.

The deeply entrenched seven-day week has not gone completely unchallenged. Notable attempts to alter it were made on two occasions in European history. In 1792 the leaders of the French Revolution introduced a new calendar in an attempt to secularize time, to remove it from the jurisdiction of the church, which had been associated with the monarchy. The French Republican calendar reform reflected the philosophy of the Enlightenment, the Age of Reason, which was ushered in with the Revolution. Based on the newly revised metric decimal system, the cornerstone of Western mathematics, it featured months comprised of three ten-day weeks, or *décades*. Each day had ten hours that were divided into one hundred minutes, each minute having one hundred seconds. Sensible though it might have been, its appeal was lost on the people. On January 1, 1806, Napoleon Bonaparte declared it dead and reclaimed the Gregorian calendar.

In 1929 the Union of Soviet Socialist Republics adopted the *nepreryvka*, a new, continuous workweek comprised of five days, each named after a color. For the sake of efficiency and maximum production, every citizen was assigned a different rest day, thus eliminating any general, shared weekend for rest and recreation. This innovation, as one might imagine, wreaked havoc on social and familial relationships. On the first official day of *nepreryvka*, *Pravda* printed a worker's complaint: "What is there for us to do at home if our wives are in the factory, our children at school, and nobody can visit us . . . ? It is no holiday if you have to have it alone." In 1932 the Soviets tried again, instituting a six-day week with numbered days this time, but nobody liked that one, either. By World War II they were back on the seven-day track.

Six million Baha'is worldwide use a nineteen-day week. The Baha'i calendar was invented in 1844 by Sayyid Ali Muhammad, the Persian prophet known as the Bab, founder of Babism. When in 1863, Bahaullah, a follower, broke from the Bab to found Bahaism, he brought the unique nineteen-day week with him. This week revolves around the Nineteen-Day Feast, a recurring religious reunion, a weekly gathering for prayer, communal eating, and social interaction. Nineteen, the mystical number of unity in the Baha'i tradition, is the base on which the entire calendar is built. Nineteen-day week, nineteen-week year, nineteen-year *vahid*, and the 361-year *kull-i-shay*. Identical names are given to the days of the week and the weeks of the year. Nineteen, as it turns out, is a very close approximation of the square root, 19.1113, of the total number of days in the year, 365.2422, thus establishing the greatest symmetry between the week and the year possible.

We, alas, stumble by the best we can, with no standard relationship between the week and the month. Some months have four weeks and some have five. A new month or a new year can begin in the middle of a week. One week can span two months. This makes it difficult for those with a weekly salary to budget their pay, and it puts a strain on businesses' bookkeeping. But there is a movement afoot to rectify the situation and restore symmetry.

The World Calendar, designed in 1930 by Elizabeth Achelis, is built on a week-to-month congruence. The year is divided into quarters, each with three months of thirteen weeks, with one day left over. This Leap Year Day, which is undated, would be celebrated as a global holiday, World Day. Each quarter, as well as the year, begins on Sunday and ends on Saturday.

In 1936 the League of Nations made a public request for proposals to improve the calendar and were deluged with two hundred serious responses. One, conceived by Edward Skille of Drummond, Wisconsin, divided the year into seventy-three months, called metos, having five days each, named Ano, Beno, Ceno, Deno, and Eno!

During discussion of such a calendric reform in 1944, one member of the British Parliament commented, "It is bad enough to be born on April 1, but to have one's birthday always on a Monday would be perfectly intolerable."

> *Solomon Grundy,*
> *Born on Monday,*
> *Christened on Tuesday,*
> *Married on Wednesday,*
> *Took ill on Thursday,*
> *Worse on Friday,*

Died on Saturday,
Buried on Sunday:
This is the end
of Solomon Grundy.

Traditional English nursery rhyme

THE MONTH

What has two horns when young,
Loses them in middle age,
And regains them in old age?

Native North American riddle

The moon's cycle of perpetual return prescribes all patterns and permutations; encompasses all possibilities. Inclusive, its orbit is

like a chalk circle drawn around the list on Sam Jaffe's black-
board:

Man
Woman
Birth
Death
Infinity

Ben Casey (television drama)

The elemental drama of the process of conception through
completion, birth through rebirth, is played out within its ra-
dius, its promise of life everlasting fulfilled. All of existence
responds to its eerie embrace and is reflected in its luminous
halo glow.

Long ago, humankind adopted the moon as its kin. As the
moon reflects the sun, it seems to mirror our minuscule existence as well. When we gaze upon its countenance, we can see
our own face transmitted back through space, and, like Narcis-
sus, we are enamored. We identify ourselves with its moody
mutability. We recognize its influence. We mimic its magical
monthly modification and apply its lessons of tranceformation
to our own devices. Celestial shape-shifter, its cycles seize our
imagination and inspire us to change by its lofty example.

Although it was determined very early on that the lunar cycle
takes twenty-nine and a half days, its exact length was imma-
terial. What was really important was to know *when* something
would happen. For this, it was sufficient to count the months.
One moon until the next bleeding. Two moons' walking to
reach the pilgrimage site. Six moons until it is likely to rain.
Ten moons of growing the baby inside before it is born. Eleven
moons of work woven into a rug. Twelve moons until we meet
again.

The counting of each "moonth" starts with the first glimpse of the slimmest lunar visage, the inaugural instant of revisibility which is clearly discernible in the dark sky. It ends when the moon disappears once again. The Sumerians called the dark days of the moon "the days of lying down." In Polynesia, people know that our silver satellite has gone back home to take a siesta. Some cultures say the moon is dead during its disappearance, others designate moonless nights as "the naked time." But no matter where it has been, the return of the first sterling crescent as it rises above the western horizon invariably signals the coming to life, the resurrection, of the moon.

The citing of the new crescent moon after sunset inaugurates a new beginning, sets the pace, the tone, for the new moonth ahead. It was traditional throughout the Middle East and North Africa for astronomers to maintain a watch for the new moon. They would declare the official start of a new month at the moment of sighting. In A.D. 631 Muhammad declared that the Islamic calendar would have twelve lunar months and that the month would begin when two faithful Muslims together have observed the first crescent from the top of a mountain or an open plain. Prominent in Arabic art for thousands of years, the crescent moon motif, the *hilal*, has graced the standard of Islam for two hundred years. Corroboration of the first viewing was also evidently important in Mesopotamia. A letter to the Assyrian king Esarhaddon, sent sometime between 680 B.C. and 669 B.C., recounts, "On the thirtieth I saw the moon. It was in a high position. The king should wait for the report from the city of Assur and then may determine the first day of the month."

Early Hebrews employed fire signals and, later, messengers to convey to the entire community the lawful sighting of the new moon and thus the beginning of the associated lunar festivals. Ancient Greek criers would loudly announce the new moon, the beginning of the new month. In Rome, a *pontifex minor* would take watch for the first moon from the top of the

Capitoline Hill. Upon seeing it, he would call out to Juno, the Queen of the Gods. The first day of each Roman month was called the *calends*, which means "to call out." The English words "moon," "month," and "measure" were spawned from the same Indo-European root. In the Korean language, too, the words for "moon" and "month" are identical.

Each nocturnal turn of the lunar wheel reveals a subtle shift in the appearance of the moon. Tribal cultures bestow upon the days of the month wonderfully descriptive names characteristic of the exact position and phase of the moon, while we, cerebral and abstract as we are, prefer to simply number them. In parts of Polynesia, the stringlike first crescent was called "to twist," and the second day was named "crescent." The third and fourth days, when moon shadows are first visible, are called "the moon has cast a light." The thirteenth day is "the egg" for obvious reasons. The third day after the full moon is "the sea sparkles at the rising."

In the East Indies, the eleventh and twelfth days of the lunar cycle, when it is well into its gibbous, or rounded, stage, are named "little pig moon" and "big pig moon" respectively, because this is when pigs exhibit an acute agitation in the eerie light of the moon and often escape their pens. The fourteenth day is "lying," referring to the way the full moon sits on the eastern horizon at sunset. The sixteenth day, "the burner," alludes to the way moonlight comes in through the doors of the houses. The "long tree trunk" and the "short stump," the twenty-sixth and twenty-seventh days of the cycle, refer, perhaps, to the increasingly shrinking crescent moon. "Going inside," day twenty-eight, is the last visible sliver. On the "inside" days, the moon vanishes altogether.

The Hindu months are based on the ancient Hindi appellations of certain groups of stars, called *naksatras*. Each month is indicated by the position of the full moon in relation to these constellations. The Chinese calendar alternates "big months" of thirty days and "small months" of twenty-nine days. The months themselves are then subdivided into mini-months which correspond to the waxing and waning phases of the moon. Each new and full moon designates the beginning of a specified term, twenty-four in all: the Spring Begins, the Rain Water, the Excited Insects, the Vernal Equinox, the Clear and Bright, the Grain Rains, the Summer Begins, the Grain Fills, the Grain in Ear, the Summer Solstice, the Slight Heat, the Great Heat, the Autumn Begins, the Limit of the Heat, the White Dew, the Autumn Equinox, the Cold Dew, the Hoarfrost Descends, the Winter Begins, the Little Snow, the Heavy Snow, the Winter Solstice, the Little Cold, the Severe Cold.

The moonths are frequently associated with and named for common seasonal phenomena: attributes of nature, animal traits, or human activities that somehow relate to each particular lunar period. Documents from antiquity mention the Moon of the Sowing of the Rice in China, the Moon of the Garlic Harvest in Incan Peru, and the Moon of the Heaping of the Harvest in the Iran of the Achaemenids, an ancient Persian dynasty. The Mayan calendar had twenty moonths. Many of the glyphs that stand for these have been translated: Mat Month, Frog Month, Goddess Month, Bat Month, Summer Month, Green Month, White Month, Deer Month, Ribs Month, Falcon Month, and Turtle Month. Cultures from various regions of Native North America boasted the Falling Leaf Moon, the War Moon, the Sore Eye Moon, the Hunger Moon, the Moon of Popping Trees, Silver Salmon Moon, and so on.

How the moonths are named says a lot about a people, revealing specific details of environment, weather conditions, seasonal occupations, diet, and belief systems. The twelve moonth names of the Omahas, dwellers of the Great Plains and woodlands of the Missouri River valley in what is now Nebraska, clearly indicate that they were hunters, focused as the names are primarily on animals: Moon in Which the Snow Drifts into the Tents of the Hoga, Moon in Which the Geese Come Home, Little Frog Moon, Moon in Which Nothing Happens, Moon in Which They Plant, Moon in Which the Buffalo Bulls Hunt the Cows, Moon in Which the Buffalo Bellow, Moon in Which the Elk Bellow, Moon in Which the Deer Paw the Earth, Moon in Which the Deer Rut, Moon in Which the Deer Shed Their Antlers, Moon in Which the Little Black Bears Are Born.

The calendar of the Omahas' neighbors about five hundred miles to the north, the Ojibwas, reflects a completely different lifestyle. Here, along the heavily forested waterways surrounding the western Great Lakes, agriculture was impractical and large prey scarce. The people thrived on the wild fruits and grains they gathered. Long Moon, Spirit Moon, Moon of the Suckers, Moon of the Crust on the Snow, Moon of the Breaking of Snowshoes, Moon of the Flowers and Blooms, Moon of Strawberries, Moon of Raspberries, Moon of Gathering Wild Rice, Moon of the Falling Leaves, Moon of Freezing, Little Moon of the Spirit.

The Ugric Ostiaks, a group living farther north still on the vast, empty tundra of northern Siberia, have produced moon names that reflect their chilly existence. Trees seem to have been prized for their rarity and the importance of their wood— less for fuel than for shelter for themselves and their horses. The list also suggests that fish and game birds are important food staples. Spawning Month, Pine Sapwood Month, Birch Sapwood Month, Salmon Weir Month, Month of Hay Harvest, Ducks and Geese Go Away Month, Naked Tree Month, Pedestrian Month, Month of Going Home While Ice Still Remains, Month of Going on Horseback, Great Month, Little Winter Ridge Month, Windy Month of Crows.

The Jewish calendar, too, reflects the prevailing conditions of each monthly period. The Hebrew months are named from the old Babylonian months, which, in turn, received their names from the Assyrian. *Tishri*, the first month, comes from the Syrian *shera* or *sherei*, which means "to begin." *Tevet*, which falls around December, normally a wet and muddy time, takes its name from *tava*, "to sink in." *Iyar*, from the Hebrew word *or*, meaning "light," is the month in which the Vernal Equinox occurs and the days grow longer.

Early Arabic calendars once aligned the moonths with the solar year. But the current Islamic calendar, adopted in the seventh century, is purely lunar. Since the moonths travel through the entire year, the names have lost their original seasonal correspondence. *Safar*, the second month, comes from the Arabic *safara*, "to become empty," referring to the granaries at the end of the time of plenty. *Rabi*, the name of both the third and fourth months, describes the time when the earth becomes green after the autumn rains. *Jumada*, the fifth and sixth months, meaning "to become hard" or "to freeze," must have once been in winter. *Ramadan*, the ninth month, comes from *ramada*, "to be heated by the sun."

Not all of the Islamic moonths are named for seasonal conditions. *Dhu'l-Qa'dah* means "owner of the truce" in Arabic. During this time, it is forbidden to wage war. *Dhu'l-Hijja* means "owner of the pilgrimage" and is the time of the annual journey to the holy city of Mecca, which is the duty of every faithful Muslim. *Muharram*, the first month, means "sacred" and is held as such with ten days of fasting in memory of Hussein Muhammad's grandson.

The names of the Dutch months are remarkably similar to those used by the Anglo-Saxons a thousand years ago. January is *Lauwmaand*, "chilly month"; February, *Sprokelmaand*, "vegetation month"; March, *Lentmaand*, "spring month"; April, *Grasmaand*, "grass month"; May, *Blowmaand*, "flower month"; June, *Zomermaand*, "summer month"; July, *Hooymaand*, "hay month"; August, *Oostmaand*, "harvest month"; September, *Herstmaand*, "autumn month"; October, *Wynmaand*, "wine month"; November, *Slagtmaand*, "slaughter month"; and December, *Wintermaand*, "winter month." The moonths of the Druids, animistic worshipers of tree spirits, were named in honor of Birch, Rowan, Ash, Alder, Willow, Hawthorne, Oak, Holly, Hazel, Vine, Ivy, Reed, and Elder.

Several cultures over the ages have devised calendars in which every month is designated by a characteristic flower. These were not business or religious timekeeping calendars, but, rather, associative, illustrative tools used for artistic and allegorical purposes; poetry and painting. The Japanese flower moonths beginning with January are Pine, Plum, Peach, Cherry, Iris, Wisteria, Morning Glory, Lotus, Chrysanthemum, Autumn Nanakusa, Maple, and Bamboo. For the Chinese, they are Plum Blossom, Peach Blossom, Tree Peony, Cherry Blossom, Magnolia, Pomegranate, Lotus, Pear Blossom, Mallow, Chrysanthemum, Gardenia, and Poppy.

For the ladies and gentlemen of the Victorian period British Empire, the flowers associated with each month were Snowdrop, Primrose, Violet, Sweet Pea and Daisy, Lily of the Valley, Rose, Water Lily, Poppy and Gladiolus, Morning Glory, Calendula, and Chrysanthemum. December, naturally, was not represented. The same tradition matched the months with gemstones, birthstones. Garnets, red as the hearth fire, are for January. Snow-white pearls stand for February, bloodstones for March. Diamonds, crystalline spring showers, are for April, grass-green emeralds for May. Agates, the blending of two colors like sex, are for June, red-hot rubies for July. Sardonyx stands for August; sapphires, blue as the autumn sky, represent September. Opals, changeable like the season, characterize October. Topaz, the amber color of stalks, sheaves of hay, and dried grasses, are for November, and turquoise represents December.

> *If cold December gave you birth,*
> *The month of snow and ice and mirth,*

Place on your hand a Turquoise blue,
Success will bless whate'er you do.

Unknown
(Nineteenth-century English)

Keeping their priorities straight, the French Revolutionary ten-month calendar named the first month *Vendémiaire,* "fine wine month," followed by *Brumaire,* "fog month"; *Frimaire,* "frost month"; *Nivôse,* "snow month"; *Pluviôse,* "rain month"; *Ventôse,* "wind month"; *Germinal,* "seed month"; *Floréal,* "flower month"; *Prairial,* "meadow month"; *Messidore,* "harvest month"; *Thermidor,* "heat month"; and *Fructidor,* "fruit month." Compared with these, our month names fall flat. Tame and boring. We have inherited our months intact from the Roman calendar, reformed and instituted by Julius Caesar in 45 B.C.

Januarius, the New Year month, was named for the god Janus, who looks both backward and forward in time. *Februarius* was for Februus, the god who oversees the cleansing of sins. *Martius* was for the war god, Mars, perhaps in deference to March's stormy weather. *Aprilis,* from the Latin *aperire,* means "to open" or "to bud." *Maius* was in honor of Maia, goddess of green growth. *Junius,* from the Latin *junores,* "young people," might refer to the fertility festivals celebrated around the Summer Solstice. *Julius* was named for Julius Caesar, author of the calendar, and *Augustus* was for Augustus, Caesar's grandnephew and heir. As if the cup of inspiration had run dry after allocating the eighth name, the remaining months were given numbers, which, having once belonged to a previous and outdated calendar, weren't even correct. The ninth, tenth, eleventh, and twelfth months, *September, October, November,* and *December,* actually mean seven, eight, nine, and ten!

Of all possible moonth designations, the ones that make the most sense to me living in the Northeast are the descriptive names given to the moonths by the Iroquois peoples—the Senecas, Cayugas, Onondagas, Oneidas, Mohawks, and Tuscaroras—the original inhabitants of the heart of New York State from Albany to Buffalo. The Wolf Moon, the Snow Moon, when the winter is long; the Sap Moon, the Pink Moon, when spring rises up; the Flower Moon, the Strawberry Moon, when the world is in blossom; the Buck Moon, the Sturgeon Moon, when summer is at its strongest; the Harvest Moon, the Hunter Moon, when autumn settles in; the Beaver Moon, the Cold Moon.

The seasonal changes they describe are completely recognizable to me. What do I know, after all, about Julius Caesar? Let alone when the salmon spawns, the kangaroo whelps, the crocodiles lay, or the yams are ripe? The native moonth names still resonate for rural people in this geographic vicinity. But we in the cities can relate to them, too. We just need to look up, set our minds on the moon, and open our hearts to its cycle.

ONCE IN A BLUE MOON

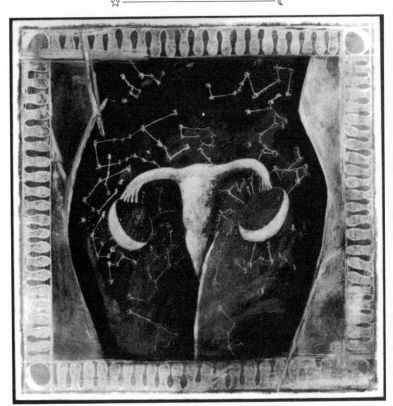

*The moon rose in all her fullness
and the women stood around the altar.*
Sappho of Lesbos
(Seventh-century-B.C. Greek)

When the moon is full, the seas rise up to reach it, sending
wild waves of enthusiastic welcome. Oysters spread their shells
wide, stretching, straining to receive it. Consume it. Swallow it

whole in the same way that they one day will slide down someone's slippery throat. Wolves howl at it. And women, with their womb waters stirred like the tides, worship it. A common connection bound in blood.

The moon is at the very heart, the core, of the universal matriarchal mysteries. I can almost imagine our earliest foremothers marking each month's menses carefully on tablets of bone, keeping track by means of these periodic tables. Certainly they couldn't help but notice that the moon was always in the same phase, the same place in the sky, each time they bled. Sister moon obviously shared the same rhythm. A symphony of fertility composed in thirteen movements, played out in lunar time. Its score, humanity's first calendar.

> & *bleeding*
> & *grazing*
> & *moaning*
> & *chanting*
> & *humming*
> & *drumming the*
> *sounds of the night*

"Dream Chant"
Donna Henes

A 30,000-year-old piece of bone found in the Dordogne region of France is inscribed with a series of notches which seem to have been made by different instruments over a certain amount of time. These notations are thought to indicate the lunar cycle. Two similar bones, both about 8,500 years old, were also unearthed—one in equatorial Africa and one in Czechoslovakia. They are both incised with repeating sets of fifteen and sixteen notches in precisely ordered intervals. The Ishango bone from the land at the source of the Nile can be read as a basic lunar calendar. It plots the pattern of time that transpires between the first sighting of the new crescent moon and the night when the moon attains its fullest circle. This prehistoric record is accurate for a five-and-a-half-month period.

Whose lunar cycle are we talking about? Whose period? The moon's or the astronomer's own? "Period" comes from the Greek for "going round" or "cycle." It means "a round of time or series of years marked by the recurrence of astronomical coincidences (e.g. the changes of the moon falling on the same days of the solar year) and used as a unit of chronology."

> That superfluyte hythe menstruum for it flowyth in the cours in the mone lyght.
>
>   John Trevisa
>   (Fourteenth-century English)

A woman's monthly blood is called *die Mond*, "the moon," by German peasants. In French, it is *le moment de la lune*. Native American peoples commonly refer to menstruating women as being on their "moontime." The English word "menstruation" means "moon change" and comes from the same Indo-European root as "moon," "month," and "measure." The Gaelic terms for menstruation and calendar are the same.

One complete moon cycle—new, full, new: blood, egg, blood—was the obvious measure of one month. People have lived solely by lunar time for most of our conscious existence. "The moon, doubtless, is the year, and all living beings," states the Satapatha Brahmana, an ancient Hindu Vedic commentary. Starkly silver as it is against the celestial abyss, the moon is the only luminary in the sky whose change of position produces a shape-shift visible to the naked eye. This makes it eminently easy to observe and chart.

O moon, O moon!
Who is your mother?
White crescent!

Elema tribe, Papua New Guinea

A lunar calendar that provides a general sense of passing time is completely adequate for the needs of those who wander. Though nomads often travel in the cool safety of the protective night guided by the light of the moon, they actually live from day to day, gathering and hunting provisions as they go. But those who stay in one place and raise their food become much more directly dependent upon the sun and its annual cycles. With the development of sedentary agriculture came the perceived need for a solar calendar. It would behoove pastoral peoples to plot the sun's course in order to be able to correctly determine the season, and to plant, tend, and harvest their crops accordingly.

The solar calendar has undergone many improvements and refinements over the past few thousand years, one of which was the invention of the month as an arbitrary, arithmetic division of the year. And so the months as they have become delineated have lost their intrinsic correlation with the real lunar phases. Calendar months of 30 and 31 days are longer than the actual period between one full moon and the next, which averages 29.53 days. Consequently, the surplus hours and days of each month, each year, accumulate until eventually there is an "extra" full moon in one month. When a month is graced with two full moons, the second one is called a blue moon: the once-in-a-blue-moon blue moon.

June 1996 was a blue moon month. In the naming tradition of the Iroquois, June 1 was the full Rose Moon and the blue moon was June 30, the full Strawberry Moon. The average cycle of the month with two full moons, the year with thirteen

moons, is 2.72 years, making it a special, if not unusual or unexpected, occasion. The last blue moon was August 2, 1993,
and the next in the cycle occurs in 1999, when we will be in
for an extra special treat—double-dip blue moons! January 2
and January 31, 1999, will both be full moons. February, with
only twenty-eight days, will have none. Then, on March 2 and
March 31, 1999, there will be two more. What an auspicious
send-off for the century. Make room for the millennium.

Rather like a leap moon, a blue moon is a great big bouncing
blue bonus. Which is not to say that it looks blue. That sort
of blue moon is altogether another phenomenon, wherein the
light of the moon appears to be tinted blue. This is actually
atmospheric pollution created by particles—usually smoke,
sand, or volcanic dust—from a terrestrial disturbance, which
creates a color filter effect. The most recent blue-looking moons
were created by a forest fire in California and the Gulf War oil
field fires.

Although blue moons do not cast an actual blue shadow,
their very existence is a celestial reminder, a message out of the
blue, as it were. A radio signal from the Great Goddess of Outer
Space to us, her very naughtiest, sometimes least sentient children. If, on the night of a cerulean moon, we close our eyes
and sit very still like a wolf, take in great drafts of air, sigh
deeply, and open our hearts, we will be able to hear Lady Luna
sing the blues. Brokenhearted, she watches down on the world,
and she weeps. One crystalline tear running down her sad
cheek, her profile a portrait of pain.

> *The moon has nothing to be sad about,*
> *Staring from her hood of bone.*
> *She is used to this sort of thing.*
> *Her blacks crackle and drag.*
>
> Sylvia Plath, "Edge"
> (Twentieth-century American)

And sister, mother, lover, friend that she is, her pain is our pain. In losing our connection to the moon and her cycles, we have lost track of our own. Like a cart with only three wheels, we are off balance, spinning out of control. We have forgotten how to live in the world. We no longer see ourselves as active and response-able participants in the universal plan, which leaves us feeling disempowered, disconnected, disconcerted, dismayed, and disheartened. Sincerely and seriously disturbed. Stripped spiritually naked and scared to death. This is not only sad, it is dangerous.

In all my years of cross-cultural research, I have never come across any mentions of traditional rituals with which to mark a blue moon. But I sense that a contemporary one is in order. I say, let us seize this once-in-a-blue-moon opportunity to trance-form our sadness into strength. Picture a perfect rite of passage into the power of positive change. A true-blue ceremony in the spirit of universal beneficence. We can start by stopping. Taking the time, noting the process, tuning in, staying with the program. Listening to Mother Moon's melancholy lament.

> Correspondence:
> *when I have sad thoughts*
> *even the moon's face*
> *embroidered on my sleeve*
> *is wet with tears.*
>
> Lady Ise
> (Tenth-century Japanese)

It seems suitable to me to strike a blue mood. A sweet, serene, sad one. Not sullen or surly, but surely a bit shaky in the face of our uncertain future. A good solid sadness you can sit with, examine, and learn from. It's quite all right, you know, to feel sad. It's certainly an appropriate response to the mess we have made. I, for one, wish to take my sadness out of my trunk. Shake it out, iron it smooth, and put it on. Wrap it around me and waltz it in front of my mirror. Wear my sadness like a baby-blue rebozo, warming my shoulders in woven comfort. But under this shawl, you see, is my ball gown or work-out suit or Wonder Woman belt.

The lights are shaded blue, of course. Blue pine incense is lit. We are bathed in an airy wash of cool blue. Dressed in our best blues, we sip some sort of blueberry infusion. Drink in its navy depths. We put bluebells in our hair. We have become like the Tuaregs, the "blue people" of the Moroccan Sahara whose skin becomes imbued with the indigo dyes of their robes. A becalmed blue aura surrounds us. We are emerged in an ocean of blue. The blue of the sea. The blue of the sky. A morning glorious blue. Just being in blue, you know, effectively lowers your blood pressure. It is known to affect the pituitary gland and contributes to the reduction of swelling and pain. Restful and calming, blue helps to balance mental confusion and ease anxiety. Hallways, lounges, and wards of mental institutions are frequently painted a pale, cool-out blue.

We cast the magic blue circle of the sky, the sea, the moon, the mood. We sit inside of it together and share our sorrow. Tell our tales; our intentions. Divulge our fears; admit our failings. The daily truths and consequences we face in the process of our lives or struggle to suppress. We open the trapdoor of our astigmatic shortsightedness, and so, let the sadness out. We wish for a better way. We wash the dirty air, the defiled waters with our tears. We symbolically clean the streams, the rivers. The ponds and lakes. The big blue sky. The very air we breathe. The entire biosphere.

I find earth not grey but rosy,
Heaven not grim but fair of hue.

Do I stoop? I pluck a posy,
Do I stand and stare? All's blue.

Robert Browning
(Nineteenth-century English)

We use bluing as our purifying agent. It's what our mothers and grandmothers bought in bottles or little wrapped cubes, to add to their wash. The same as those little blue flecks in modern powdered laundry detergents. You can buy nickel and dime size blue balls of it in a *botánica*, a Caribbean or Latin American religious supply store. Puerto Rican women put these blue balls into bowls of water which they place under the heads of their beds to promote clear dreams and visions. The antiseptic quality of the bluing cleans one's subconscious thought patterns in much the same way that Native American dream catchers work. There is a town in the Rif Mountains of northern Morocco where the doorways and windows of every single building are outlined with thick borders painted with this same blue dye. All openings and passages securely protected by concentric rings of peace.

We dip the blue balls into water and paint emblems on each other's foreheads with the cobalt paste. We anoint each other with blue blessings. I dub thee, Sister/Fellow Traveler. To have and to hold from this day forth. We pledge our affinity as cocreators of the working blueprint for a new paradigm. We pray for possibility, for a new perspective. We light bright blue candles for illumination. To show us each our own particular way. To highlight the perfect part for us to play in the exciting new epic epoch to come.

We chant for peace: Chant for peace. There's a chance for peace. For peace on earth. Chant for earth. Chant for change. There's still a chance for a change. There's a chance for earth.

Still a chance for peace. Still a chance for earth. Still a chance. We chant. We dance. We spin for peace. We slow to a stop. Stilled. Sated. Steady. Strong. The blue air is charged. We are changed. United in azure energy. Trancefused. The night is perfectly potent. Peace will prevail.

Postscript: It has come to my delighted attention that one of the participants who was pregnant during a ritual quite like the one described above has since discovered that when all else fails, she is able to rely upon the Chants for Peace/Chance for Peace chant as a pacifying lullaby. Works every time!

LEAP YEAR

☆————————————————————(

The year 1996 was a leap year. The one year in four during which there is an extra day. An extra day! What an odd concept. How in the world could there be an extra day? "Extra" comes from the Latin for "outside of, beyond." According to Webster, it means "additional to, over and above the normal." How could a day that exists and is counted be considered extra? What is normal? A year is a year is a year, isn't it?

Well, that depends. The word "year" means "period, season," from the Greek *hora*. A year is simply a segment of cyclical time. Its exact dimensions, divisions, and duration can be measured and described in any number of ways. Its turning is tabulated with reference to the sun, the moon, the stars, as well as civil and societal convention. The Jewish Talmud refers to one year for crops, one year for stock, a third year for trees, and a fourth for the measure of the reigns of kings. Our current culture recognizes and maintains several kinds of years simultaneously. There is the fiscal year, the tax year, the school year, the seasonal year, and the religious year of repeated ritual.

The solar year, which we also call the tropical, natural, astronomical, and equinoctial year, is the length of time that it takes the earth to complete one revolution around the sun, or 365.2422 days. The astral or sidereal year is the time the sun takes to return to an apparent position in relation to the fixed stars, or 365.2564 days. The lunar year is 12 moon cycles counted from one new moon to the next, or 354.3672 days. Our calendar year, which is divided into 12 months of 52 weeks and one day, is the period of time calculated from January 1 to December 31. The common year is counted as 365 days, while there are 366 days in a leap or bissextile year.

Of course other cultures have developed different descriptions of the year. Some, like the Eastern Orthodox and the Parsi, also contain 365 days, though they are not numbered in the same way. The Buddhist calendar counts 12 lunar months of 360 days, while the Baha'i year has 19 months of 19 days each, totaling 361 days. The Jewish, Islamic, Chinese, and Hindu calendars are all comprised of 12 lunar months equaling 354 days. In each case the months are of different lengths, the years are numbered from divergent starting points, and leap time/extra time is dealt with in quite distinct and clever ways.

Although people have always followed time in some general sense, it was only with the advent of sophisticated agriculture that for the first time it became necessary, absolutely essential, in fact, to develop a refined count. The concept of a calendar was crucial. The crops depended on artificial irrigation at a very specific time of the year. The same time every year—or else. The deities of the crops, the soil, the sun, the moon, the weather, had to be propitiated at the proper and auspicious times in order to ensure good fortune. And the people, separated by distance, but sharing a cultural identity, needed to coordinate and synchronize their ceremonies.

Five thousand years ago, the Sumerians, the earliest literate urban culture, developed the first calendar. Astronomer-priest-scribes devoted themselves to the keeping and predicting of time, recording their tabulations on damp clay tablets. The Sumerian year was divided into 12 lunar months of 30 days each. But since it actually takes the moon only slightly more than 29 days to make its orbit, the preciseness of the calendar was eventually undermined. Time gradually got ahead of itself.

Creating an accurate and practical calendar is an astonishingly complicated challenge which has plagued our calendrical tendencies since people first attempted to create some logical and consistent order for themselves from a universe that can be chaotic in its complexity. The difficulty is due to the impossibility of reconciling in simple whole round numbers the intersecting cycles of the sun, the moon, and the earth, which, taken together, determine the cycles of time.

One complete rotation of the earth is accomplished in 23 hours, 56 minutes, and 4 seconds. A day.

A complete moon cycle takes 29 days, 12 hours, 44 minutes, and 28 seconds. A month.

One orbit of the earth around the sun takes 365 days, 5 hours, 48 minutes, and 46 seconds. A year.

Even though the 12-month count of the Sumerian calendar is the closest approximation of the actual lunar cycle, the calendar year falls about 11 days short of the solar year over a period of only 12 months. An adjusted compensation was called for if the planting were to occur at the correct time of year, year after year, and if the seasonal celebrations were to remain in the proper season.

In order to ensure that computed time jibes with cyclical time, it is necessary to insert occasional extra time into the calendrical system. This procedure, called intercalation, can be accomplished in numerous ways. The addition of a thirteenth 30-day leap month every 3 years is one neat solution. Other possibilities, all of which have been tried over time, include the intercalation of: 3 months over 8 years, 4 months over 11 years, 7 months over 19 years, and 31 months over 84 years. Intercalation is what accounts for the inconsistencies, irregularities, and complicated confusions of the many diverse calendars that have been devised, revised, used, and discarded throughout cultures and history.

The Babylonian calendar, which grew out of the Sumerian, dealt with the situation by alternating months of 29 and 30 days and adding an extra month every 3 years or so. Calendar correction was still experimental and the results tended to be a bit haphazard. In a letter written in 1700 B.C., it is noted that the Babylonian king Hammurabi ordered the insertion of an extra month whenever his advisers noticed that "the year hath deficiency."

This clumsy system was followed for at least fifteen centuries. But by 500 B.C., the astronomer-priests had detected a prevailing order that united the dissimilar phases of the sun and moon once every 19 years. They found that 19 solar years were almost exactly equal to 235 lunar months. This knowledge made it possible to devise the first rational system of intercalation which called for the addition of an extra month in each of 7 specified years out of every 19-year cycle, bringing the total to 235 months.

About three thousand years ago, the Egyptians began to

shape their 365-day calendar. Although the Egyptians were less sophisticated technically than their Mesopotamian contemporaries, their calendar was better—at once simpler and more accurate. The year started with the first sighting of the star Sothis (Sirius), the brightest of the fixed stars. "The rising of Sothis," which coincides with the flooding of the Nile, was easier to determine with certainty than the solar cycle. Like the Sumerian and Babylonian, the Egyptian year was divided into 12 lunar months of 30 days. The extra 5 days were simply tacked on, observed but not counted. These "days of the year" were kept as a festival for Sothis in honor of the watering of the land and the start of the New Year.

In 238 B.C., the Greek ruler of Egypt, Ptolemy Euergertes, proposed an improvement to the calendar. By adding an extra "day of the year" once every 4 years, the Sothic year and the calendar year would be synchronized. But the conservative priesthood, determined to preserve 2,500 years of tradition, ignored the edict. It took two more centuries and Julius Caesar to enact Ptolemy's intercalation. By the time Julius Caesar came to power, the Roman calendar had fallen into appalling disrepair. The 355-day lunar calendar had been capriciously added to and subtracted from at the whim of the politicians to serve their own schemes. The calendar had shifted more than 2 months out of cycle with the natural seasons.

Caesar was acquainted with the Egyptian calendar—perhaps from his time with Cleopatra. And he knew Sosigenes, the Greek-Egyptian astronomer whose calendrical advice he sought. In 46 B.C. Caesar instituted the year of the great correction, or the "year of confusion," as it came to be known. He decreed that 23 days be added at the end of February and 67 days between the months of November and December, making it a year of 445 days. This set the year back in sync with the seasons. And to make sure it stayed that way, he ordered that an extra day be added to February every 4 years, Ptolemy's original leap year plan.

For sixteen centuries this Julian calendar kept the civil and seasonal year in check throughout most of Europe. But accurate as it was, it had a built-in error of 12 seconds per year, which amounted to 1 day in every 128 years. Insignificant enough, perhaps, in the short run, but by the sixteenth century the calendar had fallen 10 days behind the sun. This discrepancy was felt most by the Christian Church, since holy days were being pushed into the wrong seasons. Easter, for example, was creeping closer and closer to summer.

In 1582 Pope Gregory XIII, on the advice of Aloisius Lilius, an Italian astronomer and physician, and the Jesuit Christopher Clavius, a German mathematician, ordered that the following year, 1583, be shortened by 10 days. This returned the Vernal Equinox from March 11 to March 21, which in turn put Easter back where it belonged. He also revised the leap year system of correction by omitting 3 leap years in every four centuries. From then on, only century leap years that were divisible by 400 would remain leap. This means that while 1600 was leap and the year 2000 will be, 1700, 1800, and 1900 were not. The Gregorian calendar was made so precise that it was now accurate to 1 day in 3,323 years.

The Gregorian innovations were immediately adopted by all Catholic countries. But the Protestant nations, still under the influence of the Reformation, held out against what they considered papist dogma. It wasn't until 1752 that Great Britain and her colonies finally conformed, by which time it was necessary to drop 11 days. The same Act of Parliament moved New Year's Day from March 25 to January 1.

This calendrical correction had a profound personal and emotional effect on the population. People were convinced that the stolen 11 days would somehow shorten their lives. There were great public demonstrations at which unruly crowds demanded, "Give us back our eleven days!" The hurricane that hit the Carolinas on October 1, 1752, was widely blamed by the badly frightened country folk on the catastrophic calendar change. Imagine: there are 11 completely blank days in British and American history. For 11 days there were no births, deaths, public or private events of any kind recorded. And everyone had to change her/his birthday. In the case of George Washington, who was born on February 11, it was moved to the now familiar February 22.

Russia continued to resist the new calendar, as the Orthodox Church had broken with Rome long before the Reformation. In 1918 the new Bolshevik government removed the 13 days that were by then necessary to bring the Russian calendar into alignment with those of the rest of Europe. The Eastern Church, however, has never accepted this godless reform of the revolution. Russian, Armenian, and Greek Orthodox holidays are still figured by the old-style Julian calendar, which dates Christmas as January 7.

Today the Gregorian calendar is the officially accepted organization of annual time for civil use in every nation in the world. However, most cultures celebrate their religious and ritual year according to their original lunar and lunisolar calendars. The Orthodox Julian calendar, the Jewish, Islamic, Hindu, Chinese, Buddhist, Parsi, Baha'i, and countless tribal calendars are all still in active use. And many countries publish calendars that feature parallel versions of the year.

While these early-style calendars are kept current and unchanged, the Gregorian calendar is constantly being corrected, adjusted, refined. There has been international agreement that the years 4000, 8000, and 12,000 be converted from leap to common years. This has resulted in lessening the difference between the calendar and solar years from 1 day in about 3,300 years to 1 in 20,000. And by limiting future century leap years to those divisible by 900 and which have a remainder of 200 or 600, we have become correct to 1 day in 44,000 years! Nothing like thinking ahead.

Accuracy achieved, at least for the foreseeable future, there remains the problem of how to divide time in a more rational and practical way, and for more than a century there has been an international movement to reform the divisions of the year while keeping the precise methods for dealing with leap time. As it is, the months are of different lengths, as are the quarters of the year. The months and the year contain fractional numbers of weeks, which means that 11 out of 12 months and every year begin on a different day. This plays havoc with international bookkeeping and fiscal payment and planning schedules.

The more organized and rationalized and exact the calendar becomes, the more workable and practical and accessible we make it, the further we remove ourselves from the original goal of our task. We have taught ourselves how to tabulate time in order to be able to tell the future and interpret the past. To place ourselves. To put our lives into the perspective of its passing.

Humankind has always kept track of time so that we would be able to live in attunement with it. And that is exactly what we have lost. The more we adjust the artificial framework we have constructed for the counting of time, the more we lose our visceral, physical, emotional, sensual, and spiritual understanding of it. Our primal, personal participation in its process.

Just how long is a day anyway? How long is a night when it never gets dark anymore? How long is a month, which affects us as it affects the tides? Who even notices the moon, except, of course, when someone is walking on it? And the seasons? How can anyone even tell with all the heat-saturated concrete, air-conditioning, and the greenhouse effect? Let alone a year. How the hell are we supposed to know? Do any of us remember?

It's quite a task these days to stay in tune with real time when we have become so estranged from nature and her cycles. Perhaps we might use this leap year, the last one this century, in fact, as a sort of reality check. Use this extra day to check out this amazing universe we live in. To contemplate and celebrate the workings of our world, which, despite our constant bisection, dissection, and abstraction, remains magnificently mysterious. Let us take this time out of time,

> *To see a World in a Grain of Sand*
> *And a Heaven in a Wild Flower,*
> *Hold Infinity in the palm of your hand*
> *And Eternity in an hour.*

> William Blake
> (Eighteenth-century English)

THE NEW YEAR

☆────────────────────────────⟨

Ever since the cycles first began to be cited, since the very earliest reckonings of time, people have recognized a recurring revolutionary cosmic order. A constantly changing circular universe wherein the skies and its inhabitants—the sun, the moon, the stars and the constellations; the seasons and the weather; the rivers, lakes, oceans, and seas; and the species of the earth, minerals, plants, animals, and peoples—all perpetually regenerate themselves. Where creation itself begins over and over. And everything old is new again.

A year, no matter how it is determined, is simply a complete cycle. The Slavs and Norse reckoned years from one winter to the next. A Greek might describe a "one-winter goat." Latin cultures still speak of "a girl of fifteen summers." In Sanskrit, "year" originally referred to autumn. In southern Arabia the year spanned from one season of the plucking of the dates to the next. For the Algonquins of Virginia, the time that elapses between one blossoming of the cashew tree to the next is a year. The Dahomeys of West Africa have a term for year that translates as "time of reaping maize and eating it plus time of planting it again and reaping it again."

> *The year is at its close,*
> *A spindle ravels thinning thread;*
> *One strand is left, a single hour.*
> *And time, a glowing, pulsing rose,*
> *Will crumble as a final flower,*
> *Dusty and dead.*
>
> Annette Elisabeth von Droste-Hülshoff
> (Nineteenth-century German)

The transition, the precise turning point, between the end of one cycle and the start of another denotes the New Year. Since the world and all of its parts are always turning, there are many possible ways to calculate the moment when a year is new. And, consequently, there is great diversity among peoples as to the determination of the timing of the actual New Year.

Most cultures count the annual cyclic return according to the movements of the heavenly bodies. The Vernal Equinox was celebrated as New Year throughout the ancient Near and Mideast. Norooz, the ancient Persian New Year, has survived in modern Iran. The spring—when birds lay their eggs, plants and animals are born; when all of nature is refreshed, replenished, renewed—is a perfect time to begin a new year. On the other hand, the Autumn Equinox, when the hard labor of the growing and harvest seasons is finished and when the storehouses are filled with grains and roots and nuts, is equally ideal. The Jewish New Year begins on the new moon after the Fall Equinox. The Cherokee New Year, Nutwatiegwa, when the world is re-created, is on the full Harvest Moon in the fall.

The Winter Solstice, when the sun is reborn with new strength and the days begin to lengthen, is New Year for those who live in arctic climates, like the Koryaks of northern Siberia, the East Greenlanders, and the Eskimos of Hudson Bay. The Iroquois New Year is the Winter Festival of Dreams. In China, New Year is the second new moon after the Winter Solstice, or when the new moon was closest to the constellation Aquarius. Tibetan New Year is the full moon in February or March. The Celts and the Teutons celebrated New Year on the autumn cross-quarter day, when the natural world was in its death throes. The logic here is that death feeds life, that the new is born from the old. The Wiccan tradition still observes Halloween as the witches' New Year, Samhain.

In Myanmar (formerly Burma), New Year is called Thingyan, which means "to change" and "to transfer." This refers to the change in position of the sun from the asterism, Revati in Meen to the asterism, Aswini in Mesh, or when the sun enters Aries. The position of the star Na in relation to the new moon signals the start of the New Year in Micronesia. The rising of the Pleiades indicated the New Year to the Incas of Peru, and the rising of the brightest star, Sirius, marked that of ancient Egypt.

Other cultures look to climatic and atmospheric patterns and assorted intermittent acts of nature. In Egypt, the New Year starts when the Nile rises in June or July. In tribal India and Australia, the end of the dry season signals the New Year, and the Bushmen of the Kalahari Desert in southern Africa celebrate with the coming of the rains. The Coptic New Year, Enkutatash, coincides with the end of the spring rains and the lush greening of the land. The New Year of the Selk'nam people of Tierra del Fuego and the Andaman Islanders marks the banishment of the cold, stormy season. In Mesopotamia of old, New Year was in the autumn after the end of the summer drought.

Still others count the New Year according to milestones in the life cycles of certain plants and animals. The Greeks celebrate September 1 as their religious New Year, as it is the all-important start of the sowing season. The Kwakiutl, Tsimshian, and other Pacific coastal Indians of the American Northwest begin their year with the annual running of the salmon. The nomadic herding tribes of Siberia, the Tatars, Yakuts, Mongols, Saamis, and Chukchis, start with the birth of the baby animals, reindeer, caribou, horses, upon which their cultures depend. The Trobrian Islanders of Melanesia, as well as the Hausas of Ghana and the Yorubas of Nigeria, consider the yam harvest as the New Year.

In Nigeria, the Igbo rite to mark the end of the year, Ibü Afo, is celebrated on an unspecified day sometime in March. A council of elders determines an appropriate day each year based on their studied deliberation. In 46 B.C. Julius Caesar proclaimed, in a completely arbitrary manner, that January 1 was to start the new Roman calendar year. The god Janus, who faces both backward to the past and forward to the future, was the guardian of the New Year passageway, like a careful pedestrian who looks both ways before crossing, The first month of the New Year still bears his name today.

From the start, the Christian calendar celebrated New Year at the Spring Equinox. When in 1582 Pope Gregory XIII instituted his calendrical reforms, he moved New Year's Day from March 25 to January 1, chosen, presumably, for its proximity to the Winter Solstice. Protestants vigorously resisted adopting these calendrical changes, and it wasn't until 1752 that Great Britain and her colonies recognized January 1 as New Year's Day. The English government still starts its civil year, as distinct from the historical year, on March 25. It's rather amazing to realize that what we have always assumed to be an age-old custom is merely a 250-year-old toddler tradition, barely older than the Declaration of Independence!

Whether natural or human-contrived, any interval of rotating time is appropriate as an annual indicator. Each places us in contact and in context with the cyclical continuity of time. Each solstice and each equinox, each cross-quarter day, and each full and new moon mark the ending and the beginning of a new cycle. Each night and each day, each hour and each minute. Each rotation and revolution. Each ovulation and bleeding. Each dream cycle and each and every biorhythm. Each heartbeat, each breath we take, is a new beginning. A fresh start. Another chance. A new hope. A new year. Pass GO.

> *A year is like a life cycle.*
> *It starts, it ends, then you teach your*
> *son how to ride a bicycle*
> *But before it's over, you want to have*
> *something done.*
> *But, if you don't do something, the earth*
> *will still revolve around the sun.*
>
> Peter Vozzo
> Grade 5, P.S. 11

New Year is a return to the eternal beginnings. An annual reminder lest we forget. Back to where there is only hope and promise and enthusiastic, well-intentioned energy. Back to the original big bang backseat cosmic conception. Back to the future. New Year is the birthday of everything. In accordance with this understanding, New Year's Day throughout Asia is celebrated as everybody's birthday. Everyone in society is automatically one year older all at the same time. Older and ostensibly wiser.

The time of the Great Turning is critical, for it creates the ambient atmosphere and attitude for the entire year to come. The period preceding the actual New Year is typically devoted to reflection, repentance, restitution, resolution, and focus on rebirth. Once a year, on New Year, or on our birthday, we take the time, make the commitment, to confront our true selves. To cultivate compassionate forgiveness, understanding, and acceptance of ourselves and empathy for others so that we might truly begin a new year with a clean slate.

I never hear [the New Year bells] without a gathering up of my mind to a concentration of all images that have differed over the past twelve months: all I have done or suffered, performed or neglected, in that regretted time. I begin to know its worth when a friend dies. It takes personal color.

Charles Lamb
(Nineteenth-century English)

On Rosh Hashanah, the Jewish New Year, a new leaf is turned over in the Book of Life. On the blank pages of this new chapter, God inscribes the names of who will live and who will die during the coming year. The book is kept open for contemplation during the ten-day New Year ceremonial cycle that precedes Yom Kippur, the Day of Atonement. At the end of this twenty-four-hour period of fasting and purging, praying for forgiveness, the book is closed. The fates are sealed, and the shofar, or ram's horn, is blown to proclaim the new beginning. At the Thingyan festivities in Mayanmar, the names of children are entered in one of two books carried by the King of Gods. Those who have behaved well during the past year have their names inscribed in a golden volume. Those who were naughty are listed in a book covered in dog skin.

The New Year rituals of many lands enact a literal removal of the old year and an attendant readiness for the new. At Asura, the Moroccan New Year, the figure of the mythical being Baba Aisor, the Old Year, is buried in the earth. Similarly, in Ecuador, effigies of the old year, Año Viejo, are constructed from clothes stuffed with straw and then burned at midnight on New Year's Eve. In Laos, the goddess of the old year departs on the last day, leaving the people without a goddess or a year for one full, dangerous day before her replacement arrives, bringing the New Year with her. Today, in the West, the old year is personified by Old Man Time, who limps out leaning on his scythe. Scattering the used pages of the old calendar behind him, he reluctantly exits upon the arrival of the brand-new-baby year.

In a grand operatic out-with-the-old-and-in-with-the-new gesture, Italians throw all the belongings they no longer want out of their windows on New Year's Eve. Everything from used bars of soap to broken sofas is dispatched in this abandon; and every year there are many injuries to hapless revelers on the streets below. In a more tame tradition, symbolic of the same spirit, the Mayans replace all of their articles of everyday use. And in many Native American cultures, in both the Northern and Southern Hemispheres, hearth fires are extinguished and ritually rekindled. On Songkran, Thai New Year, birds are released from their cages to fly free, and bowls of fish are returned to the rivers. In Japan, all debts are paid.

> On jolly New Year's Day
> My last year's bills
> Drop in
> To pay their compliments.
>
> Anonymous
> (Japanese)

All over the world, houses are scrubbed and walkways are swept clean. In old England, New Year's Day was the annual sweeping of all chimneys. The expression "to make a clean sweep" comes from this New Year's custom. Everywhere, people and animals enjoy elaborate toilettes, bodies washed, dressed, groomed, combed, until they are thoroughly cleansed—often internally as well through fasting. On New Year in Bengal, pilgrims bathe in the River Ganges. The Cherokees spend the eve of the New Year in vigil on the banks of a river. At dawn they immerse themselves seven times, emerging purified and new like the year. Moroccans pour water over themselves, their animals, the floors and walls of their homes. And in Wales, children scatter water, which they have begged, over the houses of their neighbors in order to bless them.

The old year never goes out with a whimper. Worldwide, the Great Turning of the year is greeted with a raucous noise which effectively shatters and scatters any evil spirits lurking about. Jews sound a ram's horn strong enough to cause the walls of Jericho to come tumbling down. The Chinese set off fireworks in the streets and pour salt on their home fires to produce protective snap-crackling-pop sparks. Hungarian herdsmen crack their whips to turn the year as they would their herds. In Denmark, people smash all the year's broken crockery against the doors of their friends in a New Year benediction. In cities across America, drunken men gather on rooftops and shoot their firearms into the sky.

As the moment of the New Year approaches, Igbo children dash home and bolt themselves inside so that they won't be carried off by the old year. They bang on the door and wail the whole while, joining the village-wide loud lament. Tibetan magicians perform New Year exorcism dances wearing demons' masks, brandishing daggers, and beating skull drums. At midnight New Year's Eve in Japan, the watch gong rings out 108 times to purge the 108 human weaknesses described by Buddha.

We, too, ring bells and horns and sirens and other industrial sound makers, sending shrill cheers into the middle of the night for the changing of the annual guard.

> *Ring out the old shapes of foul disease;*
> *Ring out the narrowing lusts of gold;*
> *Ring out the thousand wars of old,*
> *Ring in the thousand years of peace.*

Alfred Tennyson
(Nineteenth-century English)

The New Year is also a time for the community to come together to reaffirm a positive sense of connection and purpose. At New Year we engage in an intense self-examination not only for ourselves as individuals but for the community as a whole. This reflects a recognition that personal desire for change, no matter how fervent, depends on the changes that others are able to make, and is rooted in a strong sense of collective interdependence.

But today, notwithstanding our intricately practical international technological network and infrastructure, we are prone to suffer a profound and debilitating sense of disconnection from the world around us as well as from our own inner selves. We are seized by a poignantly infinite loneliness and insidious isolation.

This New Year may we come out of the cocoon closets of our separate selves to claim and maintain our mutual response-ability and respect. Let us glory in the Numinous Nineties—a new era of conscious celebration and conscientious preservation of the energetically charged web that connects and energizes our entire universe.

BIRTHDAYS

I was born on my mother's birthday. As a child, I was absolutely enchanted by this bit of information. Did I come all wrapped in ribbons? I would ask. Were there balloons? A cake? Did the nurses sing "Happy Birthday to You" to you? And my mother, being of the glass-is-half-empty school, would reply that, although I was certainly a lovely present, she could think of several things that she'd rather have been doing on her (pre-Lamaze) birthday.

Who doesn't awaken on their birthday with a tingle, a heart-skip of excitement? A trill of a thrill, a nascent throb? The date jumps out at us from newspapers, calendars, mail, and memos, and we start the day with a stimulated sense of anticipation, or, for some, perhaps, trepidation. In any case, a heightened aware-ness of a period of personal significance. Of specialness. Our birthday is the anniversary of our self, the blessing of the fact of our being.

Birthdays have become our most basic and widely celebrated holiday, yet, given the advanced age of human ceremonial cul-ture, their observance is actually a relatively recent addition to the international lexicon of Celestially Auspicious Occasions. Birthdays, calendar-dependent as they are, are only as old as recorded time.

The commemoration of a particular day as the anniversary of anything depends upon the capacity to calculate an exact date. Many tribal and peasant peoples in the world today don't know their actual calendrical birthdays. My gramma, for one, knew only that she had been born in the spring. So she used to celebrate her birthday around Shavuot, a Jewish pastoral fes-tival. This was as accurate as she could get, as no official ac-counts were kept to document the dates of birth of Gypsies, Jews, or serfs.

The early civilizations with the most sophisticated calendars were invariably theocracies, tightly organized and ruled—the spiritual realm as well as the civic—by a divinely ordained priestly dynasty, direct descendants from the heavens. Only this gentry and the gods themselves were deemed worthy of having dated birthdays, let alone festivities. The first birthday party in history, that of the Egyptian pharaoh Ptolemy V, is described in hieroglyphic symbols carved into the Rosetta stone in the second century B.C.

The major annual festival of Hindus, Buddhists, Christians, and Muslims worldwide, even now, is the observation of the birthday of the godhead whose blessed life in each case brought about the beginning of a new age. The birthdays of the sun and moon are feted in China. T'ai Yang, the Ruler of Day, is honored on the second day of the second moon, and the fifteenth of the eighth moon, the autumn Harvest Moon, is the day of T'ai Ying, Ruler of Night.

Throughout the Orient, the birthday of the Buddha in 563 B.C. is marked by Wesak, the full moon in May. The nativity of Jesus Christ is celebrated at Christmas, three days after the Winter Solstice—a birthday that he shares with other gods of light who preceded him: the Persian Mithra, the Egyptian Horus, and the Greek Apollo and Dionysus. The birthday of baby Krishna, called Janmashtami in India and Krishna Jayanti in Nepal, is celebrated at midnight on the first sighting of the new moon in the month of *Bhadra* (August-September). The birthday of Muhammad, the twelfth day of *Rabi-ul-Avel*, the third month, is called diversely *Ma'ulid Annabi*, *Moulidi-n-nabi*, and *Damba* in different parts of the Islamic world.

Our child-centered birthday culture, a family-oriented folk adaptation of the Feast of the Epiphany, originated in nineteenth-century Germany. These *Kinderfesten* were introduced and popularized in Great Britain and the Empire by Queen Victoria, whose ancestors, governess, and husband were all German. The elaborate festivities that she organized for her own nine children became the models of modern birthday parties, celebrated practically everywhere since World War II.

The traditional, stereotypical Victorian birthday tea party, proper and sedate as it might have been, is a direct descendant of the Lenaia, the Greek festival to honor the birthday of Dionysus. These wild festivities included dances, games and songs, sweets and drink. The central ceremonial feature was a huge phallus that was paraded in praise of the god. This lingam, which symbolizes fertility and expansion, evolved over time into an equally huge Epiphany candle, which was carried in procession on the Twelfth Night of Christmas by the medieval church.

Contemporary birthday celebrations have become, like everything else we touch, increasingly commercialized, but the essential ritual elements—the cake, the candles, the wishes, the party crowns, the greeting cards, the spanks, and the singing—have remained the same through time.

Every birthday is a rite of passage. A ritual of progression through the stages of the ages. The travel from one state of being, of status, to another has always been held to be fraught with danger. Life is fragile after all, and vulnerable. So care must be taken to ensure a safe crossing for the celebrant. S/he must be surrounded by well-wishers who, with their cheerful salutations, songs, and spells of "Happy Birthday!" attempt to please the protective and guiding spirits. The giving of gifts provides an extra surety of safekeeping.

Birthday celebrants around the world are variously spanked, smacked, whacked, punched, pinched, earlobes pulled, pricked with pins, or bumped (picked up by their arms and legs and bounced onto the floor) one time for every year of life plus "one to grow on"—invocations, all, for good luck in the coming year. The birthday beat of time, tapped out in flesh. Birthday spankings are related to the use of beating, flagellation, scarification, and other painful practices inflicted upon a person in the course of initiation rites. Physical suffering serves both to purify the initiate and to underscore the gravity of the transition. Birthday hazings promote the empowerment that comes to one who can endure an ordeal.

Party games, as well as the custom of measuring and marking a child's annual growth in height, are also derived from initiation rites of passage where displays of development and the showing off of new skills and strength were celebrated. The granddaddy of all birthday games, Pin the Tail on the Donkey, reflects an ancient image of humility when confronting the magical mystery of the New Year ahead. The players fumble blindfolded in the face (backside, actually) of the unknown future, feeling their way toward their task. A reminder that we are just about as adept as jackasses.

The crown of Apollo translates into party hats and the many other ways in which the birthday girl/boy is coronated Queen/King for a Day. In Holland, even-year birthdays are called crown days and odd-year, half-crown. On crown year birthdays, the celebrant is treated to a much more lavish display. Throughout northern Europe, the birthday child is enthroned on a specially decorated chair which befits the majesty of the occasion. The Filipino child is decked out, head to shoe, in completely new clothes. National flags are flown in Denmark in honor of every person's birthday. A large apartment complex might sport several on any given day, each one the fluttering standard of an individual life. In education-obsessed Cuba, birthday kids are indulged by being allowed to stay home from school.

Since the advent of agriculture, special cakes have been offered in religious ceremony. The Persians consecrated sweet honey cakes and placed them on the altars of the Great Goddess in her many guises. A circular cake topped by a glowing taper was offered by the ancient Greeks to Artemis, the moon, in the fullness of her monthly birthday. In Japan, too, round rice moon cakes are still offered to Lady Moon at her birthday on the full fall Harvest Moon. "Happy cakes" were given as party favors at the night-long Egyptian feasts in honor of all ten-day-old babies. Emperor Hadrian of imperial Rome sent gift cakes to his coterie on his own birthday.

The modern birthday cake was invented by German bakers in the Middle Ages. Not unlike the Goddess cakes, they were ringed by burning candles, "the Light of Life," each representing a year plus an extra one for luck. These were kept lit all day long in a symbolic guardian circle until the cake was cut and eaten after the evening meal. In Great Britain, birthday cakes, like Twelfth Night cakes, contain small charms which are mixed into the batter and then baked. When these lucky pieces show up in someone's slice of cake, they tell the future of the finder: a ring for marriage, a thimble for spinster/bachelorhood, a button for poverty, a coin for prosperity, a seed for fertility.

Candles, lanterns, lamps, and torches are employed universally to light the way along the spirit path of progress. In another domestic adaptation of the Epiphany tradition, many families keep a tall twelve-year candle for each child. This is first lit at the christening, then burned bit by bit, year after year, until the child attains adulthood at the age of thirteen. A candle, of course, represents life; a birthday candle, *our* life—the spark, the heat, the glow, the movement, the meltdown, the ultimate burnout. We kindle a ceremonial fire so that the propitiatory power of our prayers can rise on the smoke, fly on the flames, find its way up to heaven. We make a wish and bless it with a blow of our life's breath, which one day, too, will be extinguished.

> *Is that a birthday? 'tis, alas! too clear;*
> *'Tis but the funeral of the former year.*

> Alexander Pope
> (Eighteenth-century English)

Somehow, especially as we grow older, cake and low-fat frozen yogurt are no longer the fulfilling richness we seek in our birthday celebrations. A party doesn't feed us; the day doesn't quite seem to satisfy us the way it used to. The promise implicit in the pomp is gone. We have seen what we have seen. We know what we know. We are left, more and more, with a subtle sense of disappointment and an unsettling reminder of the ever-swifter passage of time.

A birthday, then, becomes a time line, a life line, a party line, a deadline. An assessment of our annual bottom line. Research shows that there is a definite "birthday effect" on the health of a given group. The incidence of heart attacks increases significantly for both men and women during the week before and after their birthdays. This might be equally explained, I suppose, by the added emotional/physical stress of ambivalent anticipation and ultimate letdown and over-the-top partying. Elderly and terminally ill women, who perhaps associate their birthdays with receiving more attention and affection than normal, tend to postpone their death until one week afterward, which is the highest female death rate for the year. Men, in contrast, die more often during the week before their birthday, conceivably out of consternation at the prospect of an inevitable self-critique. "I feel nothing except a certain difficulty in continuing to exist," wrote Bernard de Fontenelle, an eighteenth-century French writer, who died one month short of his hundredth birthday. On his eightieth birthday, Tolstoy wrote in his diary, "All my life I have hated anniversaries of every sort. It's a ridiculous habit. At this advanced age, when there is nothing left to think about but death, they want me to bother with that."

A study conducted over a period of twenty-five years in a Chinese community in California shows a 35 percent drop in the death rates for women over the age of seventy-five in the week preceding the Harvest Moon Festival. The much esteemed eldest woman in a household presides over this celebration, which is, remember, the birthday of Lady Moon. A similar ability to forestall death has been evidenced in some Orthodox Jewish men who die in higher numbers right after Passover, the ritual observance of vernal renewal and rebirth and, for much of the history of Western civilization, the New Year.

Our birthday is our own personal new year. It is an annual reunion with ourselves, and attendance is required. It is a periodic opportunity to take serious personal stock. "How am I doing?" as Ed Koch, former mayor of New York City, would always ask. What have I learned? And what can I just not get through my thick skull? Like any new beginning, our birthday is an ideal time to sharpen our focus, realign our perspective, and rededicate ourselves to living the very best life we can.

"The return of my birthday, if I remember it, fills me with thoughts which it seems to be the general care of humanity to escape," wrote James Boswell in *The Life of Samuel Johnson*. Since the early 1980s, I have kept a birthday book. I usually retreat to some extent and fast to some degree during the week or so before my birthday, during which time I devote myself entirely to the recording of the past year. Processing my impressions and my lessons. Plotting my progress. Pondering my problems. Planning my goals. Ultimate good girl that she was, Princess Victoria of Great Britain wrote in her journal on her eighteenth birthday:

> How old! and yet how far I am from being what should be.
> . . . I shall from this day take the firm resolution to study. . . .
> to keep my attention always well fixed on whatever I am
> about, and strive everyday to become less trifling and more
> fit for what, if Heaven wils [sic] it, I'm someday to become!

In addition to being perfect for self-reflection, a birthday is also a time to emphasize one's connectedness to one's community. Individual birthdays are not celebrated everywhere. Rather, in many cultures people mark them communally. In many parts of the Orient, for example, the entire population celebrates a single birthday in common—appropriately enough, New Year's Day. In Korea, everyone, regardless of age, has twelve candles on her/his birthday cake—one for each moon of the year. By the New Year, debts are paid, houses are scrubbed, new fires are laid, and everybody starts the New Year together, automatically one year older, and hopefully, for everyone's sake, wiser. Racehorses, too, are all declared a year older on January 1.

Agemates are honored together in Japan in two major milestone ceremonies. Shichi-go-San, or Seven-Five-Three, is exclusively for three-year-old children, five-year-old boys, and seven-year-old girls, who gather with their families at the same Shinto shrine where their birth was recorded. Here, they are gifted with "thousand-year candy" to bless them with good luck and a long life. On Seijin-No-Hi, Adult's Day, all twenty-year-olds in the entire country are honored in a national coming-of-age party. Elsewhere, throughout the Native Americas, Africa, the Arctic, and tribal Asia and Pacific cultures, groups of youth are initiated into adulthood as a unified group, which then maintains a strong lifelong relationship.

It is still customary in countless countries to name a child after a saint and to celebrate her/his life on the name day of the patron, rather than on the child's own personal birthday. In this way, the day is shared with countless others worldwide. Of course, when you think about it, we all share our birthdays on a massive scale. Every day 8,400 Americans turn forty and another 5,500 reach the age of sixty-five. And thirty celebrate their centennials. Imagine: if you divide the approximately 6 billion people on earth by 365.25 days in a year, we each have 16,427,105 global birthday mates!

In any group of twenty-three people, the odds are fifty-fifty of having a birthday matchup. The larger the group, the better the chance. One such propitious match was discovered in 1986 by Lynda Couture of Pensacola, Florida, a citizen diplomat to the then Soviet Union, and her Russian counterpart, Olga Kostilova. The two women were thrilled by the coincidence of a shared birthday and intrigued by the creative possibilities for positive interaction which it suggested. After separating, they proceeded from their respective homes to cofound Birthday

Friends for Peace, an organization that served as a conduit through which birthday twins from both countries could exchange gifts and greetings. International sisterhood and brotherhood, indeed!

Beyond being a declaration of kinship to the entire family of humanity (may we see it flourish in our lifetime), a birthday is, by extension, an acknowledgment of our relationship to all living things. A ritual that is practically universal is the planting of a fruit tree seedling when a baby is born. The two, siblings from the same Mother Earth, are linked for life and celebrate a mutual birthday. As the tree grows, so does the child. The child, like the tree, learns to keep her feet planted in the earth and to hold his head up high. To become a steadfast pillar of the community. The tree, which was first fertilized with the placenta of the child, provides nourishment in return. It is a living calendar which computes the years in compotes and jellies and jams.

I have a cousin who used to send a living plant to his mother every year on his birthday. When she died, he continued to send them to his aunts, my mother included. The cards always say the same thing: "Have a great day. It's my birthday!"

But here is what I learned in this war, in this country, in this city: to love the miracle of having been born.

> Oriana Fallaci
> (Twentieth-century Italian)

This chapter is lovingly dedicated to the memory of my mother, Adelaide Trugman (September 19, 1914–June 27, 1994).

BIBLIOGRAPHY

☆——————————————☾

Abendroth-Göttner, Heide. *The Dancing Goddess*. Translated by Maureen T. Krause. Boston: Beacon Press, 1991.

Ackerman, Diane. *A Natural History of the Senses*. New York: Vintage Books/Random House, 1990.

Angel, Marie. *A Floral Calendar*. London: Pelham Books, 1985.

Ann, Martha, and Dorothy Myers Imel. *Goddesses in World Mythology*. Santa Barbara: ABC-CLIO, 1993.

Anyike, James C. *African American Holidays*. Chicago: Popular Truth, 1991.

Applebaum, Diana Karter. *An American Holiday, An American History*. New York: Facts on File Publications, 1984.

Aveni, Anthony F. *Empires of Time: Calendars, Clocks, and Cultures*. New York: Basic Books, 1989.

————. *Conversing with the Planets: How Science and Myth Invented the Cosmos*. New York: Times Books/Random House, 1992.

Ayto, John. *Dictionary of Word Origins*. New York: Little, Brown & Co., 1990.

Belting, Natlia. *Calendar Moon*. New York: Holt, Rinehart & Winston, 1964.

Benet, Sula. *Song, Dance, and Customs of Peasant Poland*. New York: Roy Publishers, 1951.

Berg, Elizabeth. *Family Traditions, Celebrations for Holidays and Everyday*. New York: Reader's Digest Association, 1992.

Beshore, George. *Science in Ancient China*. New York: F. Watts, 1988.

Boase, Roger. *The Origin and Meaning of Courtly Love*. Manchester, England: Manchester University Press, 1977.

Bragdon, Allen D. *Joy Through the World*. Produced in cooperation with the U.S. Committee for UNICEF. New York: Dodd, Mead & Co., 1985.

Brandon, S. G. F. *A Dictionary of Comparative Religion*. New York: Charles Scribner's Sons, 1970.

Budge, Wallis. *Osiris and the Egyptian Resurrection*. Vol. 2. 1911. Reprint, New York: Dover Publications, 1973.

Cade, Sharon. *Special Days: History, Folklore, and Whatnot*. Portland: SC Enterprises, 1984.

Calvin, William. *How the Shaman Stole the Moon*. New York: Bantam Books, 1991.

Campbell, Joseph. *The Mask of God: Primitive Mythology*. New York: Penguin Books, 1959–68.

Campbell, Joseph, with Bill Moyers. *The Power of Myth*. New York: Doubleday, 1988.

Carrasco, David. *Religions of Mesoamerica*. New York: Harper & Row, 1990.

Carriere, Jean-Claude. "The Call of the Wilderness." *Unesco Courier* 47, no. 1 (Jan. 1994): 12.

Cavendish, Richard, ed. *Man, Myth and Magic*. New York: Marshall Cavendish, 1970.

Chandris, Eugenia. *The Venus Syndrome*. Garden City, N.Y.: Doubleday, 1985.

Cirlot, J. E. *A Dictionary of Symbols*. 2nd ed. Translated from the Spanish by Jack Sage. New York: Philosophical Library, 1991.

Clifton, James A., and Frank W. Porter, III. *Indians of North America: The Potawanomi*. New York: Chelsea House, 1987.

Coomaraswamy, Ananda K., and the Sister Nivedita (Margaret E. Noble). *Myths of the Hindus and Buddhists*. New York: Dover Publications, 1967.

Doria, Charles, and Harris Lenowitz. *Origins: Creation Texts from the Ancient Mediterranean*. Garden City, N.Y.: Anchor Books, 1976.

Edwards, Carolyn McVickar. *The Storyteller's Goddess: Tales of the Goddess and Her Wisdom from Around the World*. San Francisco: Harper, 1991.

Eliade, Mircea, ed. *The Encyclopedia of Religion*. Vol. 13. New York: Macmillan Publishing Co., 1987.

Emrich, Duncan. *The Hodgepodge Book*. New York: Four Winds Press, 1972.

Feldman, Reynold, and Cynthia Voelke. *A World Treasury of Folk Wisdom*. New York: HarperCollins, 1992.

Ferguson, John. *The Encyclopedia of Mysticism and Mystery Religion*. New York: Crossroad Publishing Co., 1982.

Field, Carol. *Celebrating Italy*. New York: William Morrow & Co., 1990.

Fisher, Leonard Everett. *Calendar Art*. New York: Four Winds Press, 1987.

Forrester, Frank H. *1001 Questions Answered About the Weather*. New York: Grosset & Dunlap, 1957.

Fraser, J. T. *The Voices of Time*. New York: George Braziller, 1966.

Frazier, Kendrick. *People of Chaco: A Canyon and Its Culture*. New York: Norton & Co., 1986.

Gaster, Theodor. *New Year: Its History, Customs and Superstitions*. New York: Abelard-Schuman, 1955.

Geffen, Rela M., ed. *Celebration and Renewal: Rites of Passage in Judaism*. Philadelphia: Jewish Publication Society, 1993.

George, Demetra. *Mysteries of the Dark Moon*. New York: HarperCollins, 1992.

Goudsmit, Samuel A., and Robert Claiborne. *Time*. New York: Time-Life Books, 1966.

Graves, Robert. *The White Goddess*. New York: Vintage Books/Random House, 1961.

Gregory, Ruth W. *Anniversaries and Holidays*. 4th ed. Chicago: American Library Association, 1983.

Hadingham, Evan. *Early Man and the Cosmos*. New York: Walker Publishing, 1984.

Hale, Judson, ed. *The Best of the "Old Farmer's Almanac": The First 200 Years*. New York: Random House, 1992.

Hall, Edward T. *The Dance of Life, the Other Dimension of Time*. Garden City, N.Y.: Anchor Press/Doubleday, 1983.

Harley, Timothy, F.R.A.S. *Moon Lore*. Rutland, Vt.: Charles E. Tuttle Co., 1970.

Harper, Howard V. *Days and Customs of All Faiths*. New York: Fleet Publishing, 1957.

Hausman, Gerald. *Turtle Island Alphabet: A Lexicon of Native American Symbols and Culture*. New York: St. Martin's Press, 1992.

Hifler, Joyce Sequichie. *A Cherokee Feast of Days: Daily Meditations*. Tulsa: Council Oak Books, 1992.

Highwater, Jamake. *Ritual of the Wind*. New York: Viking Press, 1977.

Holford, Ingrid. *The Guinness Book of Weather Facts & Feats*. 2nd ed. Einfield, Middlesex: Guinness Superlatives, 1982.

Hughes, Paul. *The Months of the Year*. Ada, Okla.: Garrett Educational Corp., 1989.

Hutchinson, Ruth, and Ruth Adams. *Every Day's a Holiday*. New York: Harper & Brothers, 1951.

Ickis, Marguerite. *The Book of Festivals and Holidays the World Over*. New York: Dodd, Mead & Co., 1970.

Jobes, Gertrude. *Dictionary of Mythology, Folklore and Symbols*. Vol. 1. New York: Scarecrow Press, 1962.

Jung, Carl G., et al. *Man and His Symbols*. Garden City, N.Y.: Doubleday, 1964.

Katzeff, Paul. *Full Moons*. Secaucus, N. J.: Citadel Press, 1981.

Kightly, Charles. *The Customs and Ceremonies of Britain: An Encyclopedia of Living Traditions*. New York: Thames & Hudson, 1986.

Knappert, Jan. *The Aquarian Guide to African Mythology*. Northamptonshire, England: Aquarian Press, 1990.

Krupp, Edwin C. *Beyond the Blue Horizon*. New York: HarperCollins, 1991.

Krythe, Maymie R. *All About American Holidays*. New York: Harper & Row, 1962.

Kubler, George. *The Shape of Time*. New Haven and London: Yale University Press, 1962.

Kübler-Ross, Elisabeth. *Living with Death and Dying*. New York: Collier/Macmillan Publishing Co., 1981.

Landes, David S. *Revolution in Time*. Cambridge: The President and Fellows of Harvard College, 1983.

Larousse Encyclopedia of Astronomy. Translated by Michael Guest. London: Batchworth Press, 1959.

Leach, Maria, and Jerome Fried, eds. *Funk and Wagnalls Standard Dictionary of Folklore Mythology and Legend*. San Francisco: Funk & Wagnalls, 1949–50.

Levine, Stephen. *Healing into Life and Death*. New York: Anchor Books/Doubleday, 1987.

Lowie, Robert H. *Indians of the Plains*. Lincoln, Nebr.: University of Nebraska Press, 1954.

Luce, Gay Gaer. *Biological Rhythms in Human and Animal Physiology*. New York: Dover Publications, 1971.

MacGregor, Geddes. *Dictionary of Religion and Philosophy*. New York: Paragon House, 1989.

Magill, Frank N., ed. *Great Events from History*. Vol. 3 (951–1500). Englewood Cliffs, N.J.: Salem Press, 1972.

McGaa, Ed. *Mother Earth Spirituality: Native American Paths to Healing Ourselves and Our World*. New York: HarperCollins, 1990.

Means, Russell. Interview by John Edgar Wideman. *Modern Maturity*, Sept.–Oct. 1995.

Michell, John. *The Earth Spirit: Its Ways, Shrines and Mysteries*. New York: Crossroad Publishing Co., 1975.

Mills, Jane. *Womanwords: A Dictionary of Words About Women*. New York: Free Press/Macmillan, 1989.

Mitchell, S. A. *Eclipses of the Sun*. New York: Columbia University Press, 1923.

Monroe, Jean Guard, and Raymond A. Williamson. *They Dance in the Sky: Native American Star Myths*. Boston: Houghton, 1987.

Murie, James R. *Ceremonies of the Pawnee*. Washington, D.C.: Smithsonian Institution Press, 1981.

Myers, Robert J. *Celebrations: The Complete Book of American Holidays*. Garden City, N.Y.: Doubleday, 1972.

Neumann, Erich. *The Great Mother*. Translated from the German by Ralph Manheim. Bollingen Series 47. Princeton: Princeton University Press, 1955, 1963.

Niehammer, Carolyn. *Daughters of the Earth: The Lives and Legends of American Indian Women*. New York: Collier Books/Macmillan Publishing Co., 1977.

Noble, Vicki. *Shakti Woman: Feeling Our Fire, Healing Our World: The New Female Shamanism*. San Francisco: HarperSan Francisco, 1991.

Nordmann, Charles. *The Tyranny of Time: Einstein or Bergson*. Translated from the French by Fournier d'Albe. New York: International Publishers, 1925.

Opie, Iona, and Moira Tatem, eds. *Dictionary of Superstitions*. New York: Oxford University Press, 1992.

Palmer, Brooks. *The Lure of the Clock*. 1932. Reprint, New York: Crown Publishers, 1963.

Pegg, Bob. *Rites and Riots: Folk Customs of Britain and Europe*. Dorset, England: Blandford Press, 1981.

Pennick, Nigel. *The Pagan Book of Days*. Rochester, Vt.: Destiny Books, 1992.

Perera, Sylvia Brinton. *Descent to the Goddess: A Way of Initiation for Women*. Toronto: Inner City Books, 1989.

Powers, Mala. *Follow the Year: A Celebration of Family Holidays*. San Francisco: Harper & Row, 1985.

Ridpath, Ian. *Star Tales*. New York: Universe Books, 1988.

Rufus, Anneli S., and Kristan Lawson. *Goddess Sites: Europe*. New York: HarperCollins, 1991.

Rush, Anne Kent. *Moon, Moon*. Random House/Moon Books, 1976.

Shemanski, Frances. *A Guide to Fairs & Festivals in the United States*. Westport, Conn.: Greenwood Press/Congressional Information Service, 1984.

Simon, Seymour. *Weather and Climate*. New York: Random House Science Library/Random House, 1969.

Spicer, Dorothy Gladys. *The Book of Festivals*. New York: Woman's Press, 1937.

Still, Henry. *Of Time, Tides, and Inner Clocks*. New York: Pyramid Books, 1972.

Stone, Merlin. *When God Was a Woman*. London: Virago Press, 1976.

———. *Ancient Mirrors of Womanhood*. 2 vols. New York: New Sibylline Books, 1979.

Sweetman, David. *Women Leaders in African History*. Portsmouth, N. H.: Heinemann Educational Books, 1984.

Teish, Luisah. *Jambalaya: The Natural Woman's Book of Personal Charms and Practical Rituals*. New York: HarperCollins, 1985.

———. *Carnival of the Spirit: Seasonal Celebrations of Rites of Passage*. New York: HarperCollins, 1994.

Verdet, Jean-Pierre. *The Sky, Mystery, Magic and Myth*. New York: Harry N. Abrams, 1992.

von Franz, Marie-Louise. *Art and Imagination*. Lancashire, England: Keyspools, Golborne, 1978.

Walker, Barbara G. *The Woman's Encyclopedia of Myths and Secrets*. San Francisco: HarperSan Francisco, 1983.

———. *The Woman's Dictionary of Symbols and Sacred Objects*. New York: Harper & Row, 1988.

Wallechinsky, David, and Irving Wallace. *The People's Almanac*. 2 vols. New York: William Morrow & Co., 1978.

Wallechinsky, David, Irving Wallace, and Amy Wallace. *The People's Almanac Presents the Book of Lists*. New York: William Morrow & Co., 1977.

Warren, William W. *History of the Ojibway Nation*. Minneapolis: Ross & Haines, 1957.

Weiser, Francis X. *The Holyday Book*. Harcourt, Brace & Co., 1956.

————. Christian Feasts and Customs. Harcourt, Brace & Co., 1958.

Williams, Jack. *The Weather Book*. New York: Vintage Books/Random House, 1992.

Wong, C. S. *A Cycle of Chinese Festivities*. Singapore: Malaysia Publishing House, 1967.

Wynne, Patrice. *The Womanspirit Sourcebook*. San Francisco: Harper & Row, 1988.

Young, Serinity, ed. *An Anthology of Sacred Texts by and About Women*. New York: Crossroad, 1994.

Grateful acknowledgment is made to the following for permission to reprint the copyrighted material listed below:

Alegría, Claribel. *Search*. El Salvador: Editorial Universitaria, Universidad de El Salvador.

Austin, Mary. Excerpts from "Song of an Old Woman Abandoned by Her Tribe" from *The American Rhythm* by Mary Austin. Copyright 1923, 1930 by Mary Austin, copyright renewed 1950 by Harry P. Mera, Kenneth M. Chapman and Mary C. Wheelright. Reprinted by permission of Houghton Mifflin Company. All rights reserved.

Balikci, Asen. "Poem" from *The Netsilik Eskimo*, copyright © 1970 by Asen Balikci. Used by permission of Doubleday, a division of Bantam Doubleday Dell Publishing Group, Inc.

Barnstone, Aliki, and Willis Barnstone, eds. Poetry by Lady Ise (translated by Etsuko Terasaki with Irma Brandeis) and Lady Izumi Shikibu (translated by Willis Barnstone), and anonymous poetry from "The Cambridge Songs" (translated by Willis Barnstone and Usha Nilsson), from *A Book of Women Poets from Antiquity to Now*, copyright © 1980 by Schocken Books, Inc. Reprinted by permission of Schocken Books, published by Pantheon Books, a division of Random House, Inc.

Barnstone, Willis, trans. "An Eclipse of the Sun" by Archilochus and "Full Moon" by Sappho, from *Sappho and the Greek Lyric Poets*. New

234

York: Schocken Books, published by Pantheon Books, a division of Random House, Inc., © 1962, 1967, 1988.

Beier, Ulli, ed. "Song for the Sun that Disappeared Behind the Rainclouds" from *African Poetry: An Anthology of Traditional African Poems.* New York: Cambridge University Press, © 1966.

Bradbury, Ray. *Switch on the Night.* Reprinted by permission of Don Congdon Associates, Inc. Copyright © 1955, renewed 1983 by Ray Bradbury.

Brown, Joseph Epes, recorder and ed. From *The Sacred Pipe: Black Elk's Account of the Seven Rites of the Oglala Sioux.* Norman: University of Oklahoma Press, copyright © 1953.

De Ibarbourou, Juana and Nora Jacquez Weiser, ed. "Life Hook" from *Open to the Sun.* Van Nuys: Perivale Press, copyright © 1979.

Elwin, Verrier, trans. "Song" from *Folk Songs of Chhattisgarh.* New Delhi: Oxford University Press, © 1946.

Fallaci, Oriana. From *The New Quotable Woman* by Elaine Partnow. Copyright © 1985 by Elaine Partnow. Reprinted with permission, by Facts on File, Inc., New York.

Fenton, William N., ed. "From the New Year's Ceremony, Seneca Nation of the Iroquois League" from *Parker on the Iroquois,* Arthur C. Parker, translator. Copyright © 1968 by Syracuse University Press; used by permission of the publisher.

Francis, Robert. "Edith Sitwell Assumes the Role of Luna" from *Robert Francis: Collected Poems, 1936–1976.* Amherst: University of Massachusetts Press, 1976. Copyright © 1976 by Robert Francis.

Fox, Matthew, ed. "Oh Burning Light" from *Hildegard of Bingen's Book of Divine Works.* Sante Fe: Bear & Co., © 1987.

Glatstein, Jacob. "Praying the Sunset Prayer" (translated from the Yiddish and with an introduction by Ruth Whitman) from *The Selected Poems of Jacob Glatstein.* Copyright © 1972 by Ruth Whitman. Reprinted by permission of October House, Publishers.

Hébert, Anne. "Bread Is Born" (translated by Maxine Kumin) from *Poemes.* Paris: Editions de Seuil, © 1980.

Hixon, Lex/Ramprasad. "Everyone Is Babbling About What Happens After Death" from *Visions of the Goddess and Tantric Hymns of Enlightenment.* Wheaton: Quest Books, © 1994.

Hülshoff, Annette Elisabeth von Droste-. From *The New Quotable Woman* by Elaine Partnow. Copyright © 1985 by Elaine Partnow. Reprinted with permisison by Facts on File, Inc., New York.

Ingalls, Daniel, trans. "The Sun" from *Sanskrit Poetry from Vidyakara's "Treasury."* Cambridge, Mass.: The Belknap Press of Harvard University Press, copyright © 1965, 1968 by the President and Fellows of Harvard College.

International Committee on English in the Liturgy. " 'O' Antiphon Vespers" from *The Liturgy of the Hours*. Washington, DC: International Committee on English in the Liturgy, © 1974. All rights reserved.

Lindsay, Jack. Quotation from Petronius from *Origins of Astrology*. New York: HarperCollins, © 1971.

Matraini, Chiara Cantarini. From *The New Quotable Woman* by Elaine Partnow. Copyright © 1985 by Elaine Partnow. Reprinted with permission by Facts on File, Inc., New York.

Plath, Sylvia. "Edge" from *Ariel*. New York; HarperCollins, © 1963.

Radin, Paul, trans. "Cágaba Song" from *Monotheism Among Primitive Peoples*. Special Publication of the Bollingen Foundation.

———. "Prayer to the Ghost" from *the Winnebago Tribe*. Washington, DC: Thirty-seventh Annual Report of the Bureau of American Ethnology, 1915–16.

Reckord, Margaret. "The Journey" from *Ain't I a Woman* by Ilona Braithwaite. London: Virago Press, © 1988. (Originally appeared in *Upmountian*.)

Rexroth, Kenneth. "Harvesting the Wheat for the Public Share" by Li Chü and "Five Tzu Yeh Songs" from *Women Poets of China*. Copyright © 1972 by Kenneth Rexroth and Ling Chung. Reprinted by permission of New Directions Publishing Corp.

Rhodes, Willard, trans. "Setanke's Death Song/Crazy Dog Society Song" from *Music of the American Indian*. Booklet Accompanying Library of Congress album AFS-L35. Library of Congress, Archive of Folk Song.

Robertson, John M. Quotation from "Satapatha Brahmana" from *Pagan Christs*. New York: University Books, © 1967.

Ryusui. "Haiku" from *Japanese Haiku* by Peter Bilenson. New York: Peter Pauper Press, 1955–56.

236

Schwerner, Armand, trans. "Moon Eclipse Exorcism" from anonymous Alsean poet, © 1972.

Spier, Leslie. "Havasupai Prayer to the Sun" from *Havasupai Ethnography* 29, pt. 3, p. 286. New York: American Museum of Natural History, 1928. Courtesy of The American Museum of Natural History.

Stone, Merlin. "Ishtar" from *Ancient Mirrors of Womanhood: A Treasury of Goddess . . .* by Merlin Stone. Copyright © 1979, 1990 by Merlin Stone. Reprinted by permission of Beacon Press.

Tal Baron, Carmela. "Some Eggs Do It." Copyright © 1992 by Carmela Tel Baron. All rights reserved.

Tru Nguyen Cong. "Fleeting Life" from *The Whole World Book of Quotations*, Kathryn & Ross Petras, eds. Reading: Addison-Wesley, © 1995.

Urdang, Constance. "Because the Three Moirai Have Become Three Maries, or, Faith, Hope and Charity" from *Charades and Celebrations*. New York: October House, © 1965.

Worster, W., trans. *Intellectual Culture of the Igulik Eskimos, Vol. 7, # 1,* by Knud Rasmussen. Copenhagen: Gyldendalske Boghandel, 1929.